Singing for Non-Singers:
YOU CAN!

Finding, Growing, and Using Your Singing Voice

by Ruth King Goddard MA

©2003 Ruth King Goddard
www.JoyofMusicCo.com

Questions or Comments?
E-Mail: Ruth@JoyofMusicCo.com

10617 Holly Dr.
Everett, WA 98204

ISBN 978-0-578-00728-1

Table of Contents

Acknowledgements iv

Preface vi

Dedication viii

Part I: Why? Singing Roadblocks 1

    Chapter 1: Why Can't I Sing? 3
    Chapter 2: The Performance Delusion 7
    Chapter 3: Me? Arrested? 13

Part II: How? Singing Solutions 19

    Chapter 4: Quit Trying So Hard! 21
    Chapter 5: Thinking and Believing 31
    Chapter 6: Finding Your Musical Ear 41
    Chapter 7: Moving Into New Rooms 49
    Chapter 8: Critical Connections 55
    Chapter 9: Sneaky Tricks 61
    Chapter 10: Tie It All Together 65

Epilogue: Joan 71

Appendix A: Non-Singer to Singer Stories 73
Appendix B: Practice Opportunities Index 81
Appendix C: Common Songs to Build a Unified Voice.. 85

Acknowledgements

This book would not exist if it were not for many people, including my incredible family. When getting started writing overwhelmed me, my son Timothy Goddard, a gifted journalist, interviewed me and actually began to write the book for me. His patience, insight, encouragement, and excellent work were a wonderful spark to get me going.

My husband Paul Goddard, a gifted communicator and writer, helped me find time and space to get away and focus on completing the book. Paul is also an excellent editor and helped with the editing process. My son, Matthew Goddard, graciously gave of his writing gifts in the editing process, and continues to be an inspiration to me.

I am extremely grateful to my many "non-singing" voice students and workshop attendees over the years, who were willing to risk an adventure into the unknown country of singing. I learned so much from all of you!

Janice Christensen, Joan Gilbert's daughter, thanks for your willingness to review the manuscript for accuracy and your wonderful insights. Thanks also to Donald Gilbert, Joan's husband, who surprised me with the entire set of tapes Joan and I had made of her lessons.

Many thanks to Dan Clements, Barb Caldwell, Marilyn Glosser, who read, edited, made suggestions and comments. Your support has been invaluable. And, Dan, your formatting saved me a tremendous amount of time! Thank you!

To Dave Bury, Dr. Alan Hedberg, and Dr. Edwin Gordon, thank you for allowing me to include some of your material here. Your resources have made a difference in my personal and musical growth and I trust they will do the same for my readers.

And to you, the reader, thank you for the willingness to expose yourself to new ideas that at times may be uncomfortable. You are joining a very small, but growing minority who recognize that to sing is to be human.

The most important thanks is to my Creator and Guide, who gave me the passion to both sing and to share that joy with others. You gave me joy, you gave me a song, and I will sing for you, to you, forever.

Preface

I was on the verge of attaining a lifetime dream. It was June 1972 and I had just graduated from college with my music teaching degree. I now could do what I had always wanted, bring others the joy of making their own music as I had experienced.

In college, I was very successful in the music program. I had been a member of the select choir for all four years as well as a soloist and section leader. I sang with the choir in Carnegie Hall in New York City and Orchestra Hall in Chicago, and performed solos in cathedrals in Europe. With the choir, I had sung in the world premier of one of the most important new choral works of the 20th century, singing under one of today's foremost conductors. I had composed, performed, directed, taught, and proven myself as an able musician. Music was my life, and as can happen with success in music, I was quite the snobbish *prima dona*. Now I was ready to show the world what *real* music making is all about.

Waking up the first morning after arriving home following graduation, I noticed strange sounds, a sort of "blowing" in one ear. At the same time, I noticed as I turned my head, the sounds around me changed. Having always taken great pride in my sensitive hearing ability, this was concerning.

There were other concerning symptoms, so I had a thorough medical check-up at the Mayo Clinic in Rochester Minnesota. The diagnosis was Miniéres Disease. I was told that I was losing my hearing in one ear. They suggested I would be deaf in one ear within five years, and nothing could be done. They didn't know if it would affect the other ear, but cautioned me that at some point I might go entirely deaf.

For a young woman who based her entire identity on her musical abilities, I was in trouble. My dream was to be a high school choral music teacher. With only one ear, choir directing becomes difficult, especially at the musical level that I wanted to function. But, at the same time, I firmly believed that my Creator knew what I was experiencing and would use it for my ultimate good. I recognized this was a good time to evaluate everything about who I was and where I was heading.

As I began to reflect, I realized how shallow I was, and recognized the importance of growing into a real human being, not just a "musician." I had other realizations. One of them being the reason I have written this book.

Because I knew I was going to gradually lose my hearing, I thought that this would be a great experiment. I wanted to see if tone deafness really existed. I had heard the term a lot, and it always troubled me that there were people who did not have the equipment needed to sing. I loved to sing and longed to share that love with others.

I figured that by tracking my gradual hearing loss, I would see if it affected my ability to hear pitches. Of course, over time, I consciously discovered what I had already unconsciously concluded—there is no such thing as tone deafness. The term "tone deaf" refers to the lack of ability to sing on pitch. That ability does not have anything to do with the ears, but rather is a function of the brain. Singing is a skill that can be learned.

I began to work with adults who had been labeled tone deaf. Through this work over the succeeding thirty years, I have worked with numerous "tone deaf" individuals. I have learned much about the causes and the solutions to "tone deafness." I have seen many amazed at the new world of singing that was opening up for them. I have had individuals come up to me after a workshop and with tears in their eyes exclaim, "Thank you for giving me my voice!"

Every individual that I have worked with personally has been able to clearly match pitches and begin to learn to sing using their musical ear. Not all have been able to spend the effort that it takes to learn and master this new skill, but I have seen many who were willing to work hard gain great satisfaction at being able to participate in singing without fear or shame. A few have even become soloists, but that is not what it is about. Singing is for everyone. It is personal. It is emotional. And, I believe it is as important to our human psyche as laughter.

So, if you are one of those who feel you are hopelessly doomed to a mouth shut when the world sings, have courage! Be willing to take risks and work hard. Find a friend who also struggles with singing, and together laugh, cry, and follow the exercises in this book. With time, insight, and effort, you too can join the world of song!

Ruth King Goddard   May 1, 2003
Everett, Washington
ruth@joyofmusicco.com

**This book is dedicated to the memory of
Joan Gilbert**

**She was willing,
She put aside her fear,
She worked hard,
And she sang for joy.**

Part I

Why?

Singing Roadblocks

If you can walk, you can dance. If you can talk, you can sing.
-*African proverb*

Chapter 1

Why Can't I Sing?

Joan

On a bright spring morning in 1940, 5-year-old Joan skipped through the house, singing with joy and abandon:

You are my sunshine,

My only sunshine,

You make me happy,

When skies are gray....

She sang exuberantly, delighting in the joyous release. Suddenly, her mother, no doubt frazzled and frustrated by something unrelated, said sharply, "Stop that noise!" Hurt and confused by her mother's demand, Joan associated embarrassment and fear with singing for the first time. This brief encounter affected the way Joan viewed her singing for the rest of her life. For the next 57 years that same fear and embarrassment dulled the joy and freedom that Joan instinctively knew was a part of singing.

This early experience shaped Joan's personal view of her singing voice. She told me that as a child in school she would compare her voice with other children. This comparison only reinforced the conclusion she had come to early, that she "couldn't sing."

Yet Joan still loved to sing and she did sing—to cheer herself up, with her children, at church, and working with the preschoolers she loved to teach. Her daughter remembers, "When she was home with just family busily doing our own things, she would joyfully sing or hum while doing housework."

Joan's daughter continues, "When she was not self-conscious or anxious about the potential judgment of others, she had a truly lovely voice—very sweet and clear. But, she had difficulty matching her voice to pitches she heard." And in public, that lack was worsened by the anxiety and embarrassment from so long before. She told me, "I feel very hindered when I try to sing with the congregation at church. But even though I can't carry a tune, I sing anyway!" She also told me that she was very self-conscious in leading her preschoolers in singing.

When Joan was in her early 60's, her daughter, knowing the bittersweet mixture of joy and anxiety that Joan associated with singing, gave her a surprising birthday gift. It was the gift of voice lessons with someone who claimed to be able to teach anyone to learn how to sing—that someone was me.

In 30 years of teaching music, I have met many, many individuals much like Joan. They are individuals who concluded at some time in their lives that they could not sing. They had assumed they were "tone deaf" or "couldn't carry a tune," that they couldn't or shouldn't sing.
However, these people had something else in common. They responded to their desire to be able to express themselves in song and gave themselves a chance to learn that they were fully able to sing with joy. If you give me—and yourself—a chance, you will learn that you can too.

You may never be a Pavarotti, a Shania, or a Bono, but you will discover an amazing gift—the capacity to sing for your own enjoyment, and the priceless ability to be able to finally take joy in making your own music.

Why Do I or Should I Want To Sing?

From birth, we have all been gifted with the equipment, desire, and yes, even the need to make our own music.[1] Children naturally create spontaneous music in play as soon as they begin speaking. The seat of this musical expression in every individual is the singing voice. Our singing voice is a unique, deeply central, and personal part of our consciousness and can be as vital to our emotional well being as laughter and tears.

This singing voice, as our primary source of musical expression, is the only place where our entire being is united at the same time. When we express ourselves with our singing voice, our mental, physical, emotional, and even spiritual selves are simultaneously utilized. There is no other activity we can engage in as humans that bring together these diverse functions, joining them at our deepest core.[2]

It's Not Funny!

For thirty years I've been teaching people who thought they couldn't, to sing. I have heard many, many stories like Joan's. A family member or a classmate may criticize someone's singing or voice, they develop insecurity about their voice and either struggle when singing or stop singing all together. This is a very sad but common story.

Most people would recognize the emotional damage that can be caused by calling a child stupid or ugly, and, though it still happens, it is generally recognized by society that these are not appropriate things to do. They are destructive. Yet, it is perfectly acceptable to criticize someone's singing voice as Joan felt her mother did.

These destructive views are frequently spoken as misdirected attempts to be funny. The singing voice is a socially acceptable target for humor. We see it all the time parodied on sitcoms, in society, and in our own families: "What's that awful screeching?" "Don't quit your day job!" or "Are you in pain?" These comments are meant to be humorous, but as anyone who receives the brunt of this humor can tell you, it is not funny, and in fact, it can hurt deeply.

"Musical Abuse"

Musical abuse is a form of emotional abuse, plain and simple. Our voices are one of the most authentic things about us. We can cover blemishes with makeup, hide our bodies with the clothes we wear, disguise our personalities with forced behavior, veil our feelings behind masks, but we can hardly hide our voices!

Our singing voice is a central, intimate expression of our being. As with any intimate expression, rejection, even implied, can be devastating. When we risk this rejection by using this intimate part of ourselves, a joke or negative remark can be enough to cause anyone to avoid using, or even shut down, that vulnerable piece of our being.

Yet, this is the message many of us hear growing up. It may or may not be intentional, but it is clearly misinformed and has caused hundreds of thousands to shut down their musical growth. We are expected either to sing like paid, professional performers, or not to sing at all.

It was not always this way. For most of human history "personal singing," which I define as personal expression without any intention for performance, has been both an individual and a communal activity. It has been, and still is in many cultures around the world, a vital part of work, play, worship, and relationships. It has been a powerful outlet for grief as well as joy, and making song has been a part of most homes and communities for centuries.

Music is like a language and is nurtured in early childhood in much the same way our spoken language is learned. [3] Sadly, our culture has lost the ability not only to make music in the home, but also to pass the musical language from one generation to another.

Because our culture has lost this important skill of musical nurture, there are very few today who have had the opportunity to grow their innate musical abilities. Instead, there is a sadness and sense of loss. It is interesting to me that the only place[4] in our culture that people attempt to sing besides churches and an occasional ball game, is in karaoke bars, usually after a few drinks, which may help overcome some self-consciousness.

However, there is hope. When you gain a broader understanding of the uses of the singing voice, learn to relax and "play" for your own personal and social enjoyment, and nurture specific skills, singing can then bring joy and satisfaction, instead of embarrassment and pain.

---

1. Research suggests that "singing and speech seem very different; ... singing is more expressive of emotions than speech," that singing provides something that speaking does not . "... group singing gives ... a strong, direct feeling of social cohesion and solidarity." Richman, Bruce. (1993). On The Evolution Of Speech: Signing As The Middle Term. *Current Anthropology*, 34, pgs. 721-722.

2. Dr. Frank Wilson, Assistant Neurology Professor at the University of California School of Medicine, San Francisco, reports that research has shown that music connects and develops the motor systems of the brain in a way that cannot be done by any other activity.

Recent data from UCLA brain scan research studies show making music more fully involves brain functions (both left and right hemispheres) than any other activities studied. Dr. Wilson feels these findings are so significant that it will lead to a universal understanding in the next century that music is an absolute necessity for the total development of the brain and the individual. From Children's Chorus of Maryland and School of Music Website: http://www.ccmsings.org/info/music_child.html

3. Gordon, Edwin; *Learning Sequences in Music*, GIA Publications, Chicago, c.1997, p. 236.

4. An exception is a very recent introduction of community "sings" in some close-knit communities. Some folklife festivals are also beginning to include an emphasis on participatory singing.

Life without music would be a mistake.
- *unknown*

Chapter 2

The Performance Delusion

(If you want to jump into singing with no delay, you may skip this section and move on to "Part II: Singing Solutions." However, gaining an understanding of the following issues can greatly enhance your singing growth. If you do choose to jump ahead, as you encounter any frustration, you are encouraged to return to these pages and incorporate their contents into your musical journey.)

To Be Number ONE

We live in a culture where only "perfect" performance is valued. We can all recall fans' devastated reactions to their team losing a Superbowl or World Series, ignoring the very achievement of even making it that far. Sadly, for many, the lack of perfect achievement is failure.

When this standard is applied to singing, we can see why it is so difficult to feel good about our singing voices. When working with some aspiring singers, I find the only thought behind learning to sing better is to perform, or even become a "star."

However, if this is the only measure of a successful singing voice, no wonder so few sing! How many "stars" are there in our present day popular music scene? Compare that number with the population of the U.S., and you can see that the fraction that actually "makes it" is incredibly tiny. Does this mean that those who don't succeed professionally shouldn't sing? Of course not!

Don't get me wrong; it's not that the pursuit of musical success is hopeless, but that our cultural view of musical success is not realistic. To be a "star" there are many facets that must come together. I am not suggesting that anyone give up the pursuit, but rather than focus on fame as the illusive test of success, you can focus on being the very best you can be and be sure to have a good time while you are growing.

Nero Was a Famous Singer?

A story is told about Nero,[1] the Roman ruler famous for madly playing his violin while his city burned. It is said that he took great pride in being an excellent singer and took every opportunity to demonstrate his "talent."

The problem was that, though he believed he had a beautiful voice, history tells us he was not able to stay on pitch, and therefore, it was very difficult to listen to him. Nevertheless, because he thought he was such a great singer, and was emperor of the known world, he would demand an audience.

One particular instance tells of what he planned as his ultimate triumph. He was going to sing an entire "opera" by himself. This particular piece was said to have lasted at least 4 hours. He had his soldiers posted at all the exits so no one could leave. As time went on the desperate audience feigned all sorts of emergencies and attempted to sneak out, just to escape the ongoing discomfort of listening to an attempt to sing "beyond his means."

I imagine that Nero, who we know was not emotionally stable, had "delusions of grandeur" concerning his singing ability. Any ruler who was worshiped as a god would have to be a perfect performer, wouldn't he?

Our culture has taught us, like Nero, to believe that the only value of singing is in performance. Most of us are not megalomaniacs who can or would force others to listen to us. Therefore, it is important to understand that singing has significant personal value, separate from performance.

Personal Music vs. Performance

Our singing voices are not designed primarily for performance. Singing, like speaking, is first participatory and for personal expression. Do we cringe at the "quality" of a few individuals' voices that are yelling exuberantly at a basketball game? Of course not! (Unless, of course, they are cheering for the opposing team!)

For centuries, singing has been both a community and individual expression. To only make music for performance, is as absurd as asking someone not to speak because the quality of their voice does not measure up to society's standards for a public speaker.

We recognize the right everyone has to have his or her say in conversation. However, we might become fairly irate if an individual felt that they alone should be heard, and everyone else just listen (remember Nero?), especially if we also feel we have things to say on the topic.

In the same way, I believe that the singing voice is not primarily given for the purpose of performance. Performance around the world is only a small facet of singing. Rather, I believe we were designed to sing as a major avenue of individual expression, both in community and on our own.

I remember going to community "sings" when I was growing up. We had a wonderful time with a large cross-section of ages by gathering to sing good, old, silly, and sentimental songs. There was no competitive atmosphere but instead a relaxed, informal "recreational" setting. I know as I was singing, I was not listening to others, but instead I was enjoying joining in with the rest of the crowd. We were having fun!

There is a vast difference between singing for enjoyment and singing for performance. Each has value and a significant place in both community and personal life. If you have a deep desire to be a "star," then be willing to make the sacrifices and work very hard because the competition is stiff, but go for it!

It has been said by vocal coaches and teachers on Broadway, that it takes seven years to make a singer. That is probably realistic. To "make it" takes a tremendous amount of hard work, excellent contacts, the will to not give up, willingness to look foolish and fail, and time.

There has been a popular television program where the statement is made to several "star" hopefuls: "You should never sing again." Many of those who received this "professional advice" did not really sound that bad, though they were clearly not ready to sign a record contract. That statement reveals an incredibly narrow and ignorant view of what singing is all about. This attitude has also led us to believe that if I sing by myself in the presence of others, I am performing, and therefore, should be "perfect."

However, you may conclude that you really have no desire for fame or feel it is not a sensible goal. I hope by now you can conclude with me that our cultures' exclusion of "personal music" is destructive to a great source of joy. It is extremely appropriate and natural to desire to sing for our own enjoyment. If you would like to learn how to express yourself in song without feeling fearful or ashamed, then keep reading. You are on the right track!

Electronic Perfection

Since the 1920's, thanks to new technology, anyone with a radio or phonograph could fill his or her environment with the music of professional musicians. This began the development of what I call the "fantasy tonal ideal" that has been a major contributor to shutting down our culture's personal singing.

Just as, through magazines, television and movies, women (and to a lesser extent, men) are hounded by a "fantasy body ideal," an ideal impossible to realize, the same is true for our singing voices. The singing voices that surround us create a model of what we feel our voices should sound like, but the voices of today's recording artists are not necessarily natural.

The recordings we hear are dubbed and acoustically altered – mistakes are corrected, vocal slip-ups replaced and the vocal quality is enhanced. To record a song may take days or even weeks producing perfect "pieces" which are deftly woven together by sound engineers into one complete performance.

A recent student came to me thinking that she couldn't sing but wanting to very much. As I began to work with her, I discovered she had a great ear! I could also see she was not intimidated by our culture's "tonal ideal." I then learned that even though her father belittled her when she sang for fun, she would just hide and practice singing with her favorite recordings, and loved it. This is how she developed her "ear," even though her father's words had a negative impact on her image of her voice.

I soon discovered that her father was a recording engineer. She remembers going to the studio and listening for hours while recordings were being made. As a child, she realized that a recording was not really a true representation of a voice. She heard the reality of the mistakes and distorted sounds that making a recording can mask, and so she wasn't fooled into thinking that she "ought" to sound a certain way.

Even though the image of her personal voice was distorted at home, she was able, privately, to sing with popular recordings, absorb what was attainable and, without realizing it, develop a good ear for singing.

Many vocalists today just "lip-sync" the recording studio version, because their "sound" is so dependent on expensive technology. In addition, performers have the privilege to spend time and money to build their voices. Their voice is the source of both identity and income. As a comparison, consider ice skaters – those who skate professionally have more time and financial support to refine and improve their style. Does that mean no one else attempt to ice skate for their own enjoyment?

The Gifted Few

At the same time, our culture has been embracing this "fantasy tonal ideal," changes were happening in the emphases of musical training. As an example, during the 1920's, Harvard University Music Professor Archibald Davison took over the Harvard Glee Club—a group designed for fun, recreational singing[2] — and changed it into a group of "artistic" performers. He was lauded as the founder of the American music education movement of the 20th century.

Out of a desire to develop a high level of artistry that could rival our European counterparts, music education became focused on finding and nurturing the "talented" few for high quality, artistic performance. Europe was considered the source of the finest musicians and musical artistry, and there was a concern that the artistic reputation of American musicians must be raised to better compete or compare with the well-established European artistry.

The forces behind the music education movement had no way of knowing the effects that radio and recordings would have on our expectations for the sounds of individual singing. No doubt, the assumption was made that people would always sing recreationally, and therefore there was no reason to nurture that.

As music education focused primarily on the gifted, the ridicule of the voices that were less than perfect grew. It is no surprise that many would become intimidated in singing even in front of family. What had been a skill learned at mother's knee, became an exclusive arena for the "talented" few. Succeeding generations began to lose the ability to nurture singing in the next.

The Cost of an Ego

If this wasn't enough, some of the models of music teaching that the academics endorsed were abusive in nature. We've all seen the stereotypical music teacher on television or movies, who flies into a rage if the student makes an error. It has become acceptable to use shame, rage, or other destructive methods to "motivate" students to correct errors in musical training.

I have been teaching music to individuals and groups for over 30 years and believe that for the most part, no one wants to make a mistake when making music. This is especially true when an individual is singing or playing solo for a teacher or audience. A mistake is not an act of rebellion requiring stern correction. Rather, a "mistake" is a cue for the teacher to know better where to help the student grow in their skill.

Sadly, there are conductors, directors and even school music teachers who take great pride in not allowing "mediocrity," but at the same time do not know how, or are not willing to help individuals gain new skills. It is not unusual for a "successful" or aspiring conductor or teacher put heavy pressure on students to perform "perfectly," only for the gratification of their own ego, or for their institution.

Though this abusive approach is an easy trap to fall into, those of us known as "perfectionists" in our teaching and conducting must take responsibility for our student's "mistakes." If there is a problem in the music, we must do our best to give the performers the skills and confidence needed to make music at the level that we desire.

1. Paul Harvey's "The Rest of the Story" 11/22/02

2. Archibald Davison, Music Education In America; Harper & Brothers, New York, 1926, flyleaf.

One man's critic is another man's compliment.
- ems

Chapter 3

Me? Arrested?

The Myths

There's a problem with the terms "tone-deaf" or "monotone" — they are myth. Contrary to popular belief, everyone is born with all the equipment needed to sing. The fact that we feel we can't sing is not because we are stupid, or deficient in some way. Rather it is because we have not had either the opportunity or environment to grow in musical skills.

In contrast, the "talented" are generally either those who received a lot of musical encouragement and interaction early in life, or those who have the personality that does not allow other's criticism to impact them and they have been willing to work hard to acquire skills.

The highly successful actor and singer, Will Smith, has made the statement that he "doesn't have anything that anyone else doesn't have." Instead, he states that he just doesn't "care what people think" of what he does, and is willing to take risks along with hard work.

Anyone *can* sing. It is never too late to learn these skills.[1] It is time to let go of our culture's "fantasy tonal ideal," and begin to explore our own voices. We all are built to sing and, perhaps most importantly, tone deafness is a myth. If a person can speak language with culturally appropriate inflections, they are *not* tone deaf or monotone. It is as simple as that.

Most Asian languages, Mandarin Chinese, as an example, are tonal—that is, a word means something different depending on the pitch on which it is spoken. If there were such a thing as "tone deafness," then some number of Asians would never be able to speak their language!

Only in our performance-oriented American culture do we have such a broad population of so-called "non-singers." In most cultures not yet impacted deeply by our culture, almost everyone sings for enjoyment. In those cultures, singing is an important social, relational and community phenomenon. It is only in this American culture that we have separated the musical "haves" from the musical "have-nots," and have actually created a tonally illiterate culture.

The Crisis-Moment

For many individuals, this separation can come as a result of a 'crisis-moment.' A singing 'shut-down' can happen at any age, but it usually occurs during childhood from approximately kindergarten to 8th grade[2]. Joan's "noise" is one example, and another could be a music teacher giving a specific child a "non-singing" task when the rest of the group is singing.

Any time a vulnerable individual, such as a child, concludes that they are poor singers their entire musical development can shut down. Usually, the triggers for this conclusion are not at all intentional, but nevertheless as children, our perceptions are our truth.

Sometimes it isn't even what someone says, but what he or she doesn't say. A lack of positive comments can be just as damaging as the presence of negative ones. There are many of us who, when we don't hear positive, immediately assume the negative. This lack of positive feedback has caused many to conclude they are only making "noise" and can't sing.

"Arrested Musical Development"

Whether triggered by a specific moment or years of neglect, it is these negative influences that are, in my experience, the major cause of "arrested musical development," a much better term for what is usually called "tone deafness."

Many of these "non-singers" have come to me throughout my years of teaching voice. Like Joan, they are usually embarrassed, often encouraged by supportive family and friends, and usually come apologetically. I've often heard them say that they "just want to learn to sing well enough so it won't cause pain for others."

When I begin to ask about their desire to sing, I invariably find that it is a "secret" desire, felt deeply, and connected with a tremendous amount of fear, sadness, and shame. Though appearing trivial to some, the emotional anguish these people feel, being torn between the innate desire to express themselves through singing and the "truth" they are bad singers, can be immense.

Feeling the Sadness

When Joan first came into my studio a few years ago, she came with great fear and embarrassment. All she knew was that something she deeply desired was beyond her reach.

As I do with all of my students who identify themselves as non-singers, I began the lesson by talking through much of what I've already covered here. I explained how all people are born with the equipment to sing, and singing, like speech, is a language that must be nurtured. I also described the intimacy and vulnerability of the singing voice.

Joan was very excited to hear there were external reasons that she "couldn't sing" and was enthusiastic to learn more. I then moved on, and explained to her the concept of the "crisis moment."

I asked, "Joan, can you remember a time in your life when someone said something to you that made you feel you shouldn't sing anymore?"

Joan quietly thought for a little while, and then told me about the event with her mother. As she spoke, she began to realize the profound impact that had been left when, as a five-year-old, she concluded that her singing was actually unwanted and ugly noise. She was surprised at the emotions that surfaced with the memory. As she was describing the situation, tears began to appear in her eyes and her voice wavered.

"How did you feel, as a little five year old girl, hearing that your expressions of joy were considered to be noise?" I asked.

"I was devastated," she said, "I didn't understand why my mother was saying this

Chapter 3: Me? Arrested?

to me. It hurt me deeply and I think I felt a part of me die that day."

"You were singing out of joy and love," I pointed out, "and when it felt like your mom rejected your singing, it was like she was rejecting your joy and love."

Joan nodded vigorously. "Yes, that's how I felt!"

We talked for a while about this, and as commonly happens, more tears came. Because the human voice is such an integral part of the whole person, its arrested development is usually tied to grief and emotional pain.

I spent time with Joan, helping her to see that she had interpreted the event with a child's perception—that what she perceived her mother had said was not true, and the hurt her mother had caused was not intentional. Memories filtered through the lens of childhood have a tendency to be exaggerated, but that does not change the reality and validity of their pain.

If any of this strikes a chord with you, if you have thought that you were unable to sing for most, or all, of your life, then I hope to help you. Maybe you have a crisis-moment similar to Joan's buried in your past. Think on that.

Practice Opportunity #1: "Processing the Pain"

Think back in your past and look for events that may have led to your initial musical shut down. For most, it was sometime during their childhood, after the age of five and before high school, but for others it may be any time.

If you don't remember anything immediately, don't worry about it—it can take time to identify long buried memories.

But also remember the possibility that there is no one defining moment that signaling the stopping or slowing of your musical development. It could have been caused by a complete lack of positive feedback. If you feel that is the case, try to remember a specific time you concluded you couldn't or shouldn't sing or weren't musical.

Whatever the cause, it may take some time to work through these issues. Don't rush any of this, for the whole experience is a process, never a quick fit.

Thinking about these hurts will likely also bring a fair amount of emotional pain. It did for Joan and for nearly all the people I have worked with in this area.

Don't be afraid of this—these emotions are valid and real. You may want to find a friend who can listen and affirm the validity of your feelings. By dealing with them, you move much farther along the journey to singing with joy.

Become a Child Again

Because arrested musical development usually begins in childhood, to break out of it you need to identify with the child you were, both emotionally and musically. That's why these childhood emotions may need to be felt, and why the exercises and techniques that I use may at times seem childish. You might need to "start over," in a sense, beginning again at the stage you were at when your musical development slowed or stopped.

However, be encouraged that as an adult, the growing process will take place if you are willing to work at it![3] Joan would say: "I think this is easier for me now as an adult. I have more 'pegs' to hang this new information on." In addition, throughout her life she had absorbed a "catalog"[4] of sounds and melodies, which were stored deep in her psyche.

By feeling some of the same feelings you felt as a child, you are acknowledging their validity and therefore, by processing them, can begin to let them go. You can destroy the beliefs that caused you to shut down musically by replacing them with new truths that are actually based on reality, such as "I now have all the equipment I need to learn to sing for joy." Or "I am an intelligent, capable adult, and I am learning how to sing for joy!" Or "I can do it!"[5]

In this reliving, you may find a new freedom to enjoy your "childish" adult feelings. Nurture those feelings. They are a part of the release that will help you let go and sing. So begin to learn as a child, play as a child and, perhaps most importantly, lose all your inhibitions and *relax* like a child.

1. Osgood, N.J. (1993) Creative activity and the arts: Possibilities and programs. IN: *Activity and aging: Staying involved in later life.* Kelly, J. R., Ed. Sage Publications, Inc, Newbury Park, CA, US. pp. 174-186.

2. It is interesting to note that these are the years that most children are subjected to a peer-dominated environment at school, where, until recently, bullying has been thought of as innocuous, "normal" child's play.

3. See Appendix A: "Non-Singer to Singer Stories"

4. Gordon, Edwin. *Learning Sequences in Music.* GIA Publications, Chicago, c.1997, p. 235.

5. See Chapter 5: "Thinking and Believing"

Part II

How?

Singing Solutions

Practice makes POSSIBLE
- Susan Colla[1]

Chapter 4

Quit Trying So Hard!

Once Joan began to understand when and how her vocal development stopped, she was able to begin it again. As I listened to her sing, showing me what she had been doing for those years, I understood why.

Joan, like nearly all who have not been nurtured musically but nonetheless want very badly to sing, was trying too hard. This usually took the form of tightening up the throat, in an attempt to "make something happen."

Play!

A young child internalizes language skills in the context of freedom, acceptance, and play. Learning and internalizing musical skills happens in just the same way. Can you imagine a child of two or three being taught language skills by being required to repeat a set of drills, by being shown how to pronounce one sound at a time, and then drilling on that? Or even more absurd would be requiring a child to learn how to read before they speak. Yet, that is the manner in which our culture has traditionally thought music was learned.

How many of us as children tried to learn to play a musical instrument? We were given the instrument, shown how to hold it, how to make a sound, but then immediately, before any experimentation, any play, and most importantly, any listening or tonal work, began to learn to play by reading one note at a time.

This process has been successful for many, but at the same time, I venture that at least twice as many have become discouraged or bored and quit. You may have been one.

Would you have been more motivated, as well as developed a more musical sound and manner, if you were allowed to "play" and experiment on the instrument? For centuries, folk instrumentalists and vocalists have learned their skill by listening to, imitating, and playing or singing along with an older, more experienced musician. For centuries, this process has achieved incredible technical ability.

In fact, thousands of individuals today are successful musicians in "garage bands" having never had a lesson, but having learned their skill in the context of play and experimentation.

Music, just as language, is best learned in informal play, when there is no fear of experimentation, of making "mistakes," where loving interaction nurtures a sense of confidence, where joyful practice is modeled throughout daily living. Musical skills are leaned in play, so play!

Don't be afraid to experiment, to sound silly, to experience new and strange sound sensations. Enjoy the process, interact with others (such as children) as you experiment with your "musical ear" and you will find yourself growing in understanding, skill, and joy!

Cease Your Striving

The tightness Joan was experiencing as she tried to sing came out of her great desire to do something she thought was beyond her reach. When we want to do something that we can't do well, we either give up, or try harder. Joan consciously gave up, but at the same time, the innate need to sing was there and singing became fearful, difficult work.

This "hard work" created in Joan a high level of tension, especially in her throat. Any tightness in the throat or jaw will distort the sound of the singing voice. This is one of the reasons why relaxation is such an important key to singing.

The throat is only an open channel for the air. The vocal cords work involuntarily in response to signals in the brain. No effort at all needs to take place in the throat. To learn to relax this area is critical to developing a pleasant, natural singing voice.

There's a deeper purpose for relaxation, however. I believe that humanity was created to sing with freedom and release, and we are physically and psychologically built to do so. Stress is the antithesis of this release. When we internalize our stress, it's very difficult to have this release, or to sing for joy. It is important that those who want to sing learn how to relax purposefully and intentionally.

Stress ⟶ Tension ⟶ Distortion

To understand a little more about why relaxation is so important to singing, think a little bit about where we in American society carry most of our tension. We live in what I call an "upper-trap culture." That is to say, many of the activities we put energy into tend to draw the most intensity from the upper trapezius muscles of our upper back and neck.

Typing, writing, driving, wiping, stirring, lifting, etc. all use these muscles. These are the muscles you may feel tight when you're ready for a good shoulder rub. We carry so much of our life's tensions in those areas that it doesn't take much for the tightness to radiate across the shoulders and up into the neck at the base of the skull and into the jaw, throat and base of the tongue.

Obviously, these are some of the most important areas to the process of singing. Without release in these areas, the playful experimentation necessary for musical development can be difficult.

Don't Be Afraid

In addition, long-term, continued stress can cause a body to remain in the state of "fight or flight," our body's response to danger. The abdomen becomes rigid; shoulders thrust forward; all muscles tighten as if to ward off a blow. It is amazing how many of us actually live every day in this kind of stress-focused body.

Beyond the societal causes, most who have stopped developing musically (as well as many who have not) associate music with pressure to perform and a fear of failure or rejection. This increases the tension and constriction of the throat and other areas, which distorts the sound and further discourages that person from singing, continuing the destructive cycle.

From Stress to Rest

Relaxation does more than simply relieve tension. It can actually make singing easier and sound better as well. Relaxing increases circulation and blood flow in the functioning parts of singing: the brain, the muscles of the head and throat plus the diaphragm, increasing their health and effectiveness.

Relaxed breathing also opens the resonating areas in the head, throat and chest, giving the voice a full, richer sound. This relaxed breathing is the same "cleansing breath" used in many Asian cultural disciplines such as yoga.

This relaxed, deep breathing is what takes place as we experience a refreshing sleep. However, most of us cannot easily use this breathing when we are awake. It must be learned. Just as difficult as it is to obey the command "don't think of a pink elephant," when we try to breath deeply, we may become tense and only breath shallowly.

The Breath of Rest

Right now, take the deepest breath you can. As I suggested above, like most people, you probably raised your chest and shoulders in an attempt to expand your lungs. However, that is very shallow breathing that only used a small portion of our lung capacity.

When you suck in your gut, your diaphragm pushes up on the peritoneal cavity that holds the heart and lungs, giving the lungs a great deal less space for air. In addition, when you inhale this way, the muscles doing the work are those same upper trapezius muscles that are already stressed enough by daily activity.

Shoulders do not rise in relaxed breathing—in fact, they have nothing to do with the fundamentals of breath. The diaphragm, chest, and even back expand outward, not contracting, in an effective inhaled resting breath.

To learn how to breathe effectively in singing, it helps to start by learning how to breathe in the most relaxed manner possible. Here's an exercise to help you with that.

Practice Opportunity #2: "A Place of Rest"

1. *Close your eyes and picture the most beautiful, restful space you can imagine. It may be a lush garden, the ocean shore, or a special place created in your imagination.*

2. *Stay in that imaginary space for a while, soaking in the variety of colors in an array of textures, the scents, sounds, and sensations. There are no pressures on you here, no responsibilities, simply rest.*

3. *Slowly and deeply, breathe in the richness. Quiet your thoughts to just take in the beauty and serenity of your space.*

4. *When you are feeling that deep effortless breath, continue breathing, as you try to memorize what you are experiencing physically. Stay with that relaxed, deep breathing as long as you need, allowing your body to do the breathing. Your only thoughts should be rest, and learning from your resting body.*

5. *Only when you begin to grasp the physical sensations and can begin to internalize them, slowly return to the present and resume reading.*

The deep, full breathing you just experienced, most likely through the nose, I call the "resting breath." It is the key to relaxation, which is, in turn, the key to singing. This is how you should be breathing before, during and after you sing.

As I stated earlier, this breathing is not a voluntary action. Our bodies only naturally breathe this way when we are in a deep, restful sleep.[2] Unless we consistently practice, try as we may, we cannot "make" ourselves use this type of breathing. It takes time and frequent, uniform repetition to make this type of breathing something we can choose to do.

Perfect Practice Makes Perfect

Research shows that in order for any behavior or action to become automatic or routine, it must be done daily over a period of twenty-one consecutive days. Therefore, if you practice resting breath exactly the same way for about 8 minutes for 21 days, you will be able to use this resting breath whenever you choose.

Spending eight minutes every day, stopping all activity and doing the above activity can be a key to a joy-filled singing life. If you aren't able to do it every single day, but two or three times a week or so, you will still be able to train your body in this manner, though it will likely take longer. A wonderful doctor[4] taught me this method of breathing many years ago when I was dealing with many different physical problems, and it has helped immensely, both physically and musically.

Letting Go

The second vitally important aspect of relaxation is the ability to relax specific areas and muscle groups. In order to release the tensions of the throat that can distort the tone, I use a well-known technique called "progressive relaxation," and the steps are outlined below.

Just as practicing the resting breath teaches you how to relax purposefully, the following exercise teach you how to relax both purposefully and in specific parts of the body—including those most directly related to singing.

Practice Opportunity #3: "Progressive Relaxation"[5]

Find a comfortable position that is restful. (Lying on your back, knees up, with a rolled towel under your neck, is an excellent position.)

Use the imagery exercise (Practice Opportunity #2: A Place of Rest) to remind yourself of the resting breath. When you feel you are experiencing deep refreshing breaths, you may begin.

Use these next four steps for each specific muscle group you will now learn to relax:

STEP 1. Take deep, relaxed breath, hold your breath and pull the muscles tight in the specific muscle group for several seconds ... feel the tension, focus on the sensation of tightness.

STEP 2. After several seconds of tension, relax very slowly as you release your breath and begin to breath deeply again... feel the release... sink deeply into whatever is supporting you... feel the muscles continue to release.

STEP 3. With each muscle group, memorize the sensations of release, continuing to feel the "layers" of tension melt away.

STEP 4. As you relax specific muscle groups, memorize the sensation of the relaxed muscle.

Now continue through each muscle-group as outlined below. For each muscle group repeat the four steps. Be sure you allow for full muscle release for each muscle group before you go on to the next muscle group on the list.

<u>*Remember that release comes in "layers."*</u> *An initial focus on relaxing may only be a superficial letting go and relaxation feeling. This initial release is not necessarily full relaxation. Therefore, continue to practice the four steps of relaxation, learning how to take yourself into the fullest level of relaxation and release possible.*

READY TO BEGIN:

Begin the progressive relaxation exercise with the feet and the toes. Then move up the body isolating various and specific muscle groups, taking time with each muscle group to achieve a deep release of all tension. Follow the progression from one muscle group to the next using the sequence below.

As you progress from your feet and toes to the next muscle group, imagine all of the bodily tension moving down your body and legs, and finally leaving your body through your feet as if the tension was evaporating.

Follow this outline of muscle groups. This exercise works best if you start in the lower extremities and gradually moving from one muscle group to the next, always imagining the tension flowing out of your body through your legs and out your feet.

BEGIN:

1. *Curl your* **<u>feet toes downward</u>** *until the muscles are tight and you feel it all the way up through the thighs...hold...let go...relax*

2. *Tighten the* **<u>leg muscles from the hips, knee and calf, one</u>** *leg at a time...hold...let go...relax.*

3. *Tighten your* **<u>buttocks</u>** *...hold...let go...relax.*

4. Push **stomach muscles out** as though you were going to be hit and are protecting yourself...hold...let go...relax.

5. Pull **stomach in and up** until the diaphragm feels pressure...hold...let go...relax.

6. Clench **both fists**...hold...let go...relax.

7. Stiffen **the arms from the shoulder to the hands**...hold...let go...relax.

8. Bend the arms upward and tighten the **biceps and triceps**...hold...let go...relax.

9. Tighten the muscles in **upper chest**, just below the neck...hold...let go...relax.

10. Tense the muscles of **upper back**, just below the neck...hold...let go...relax.

11. Pull **shoulders** up to ears. Feel the tension in back and chest...hold...let go...relax.

12. **Shorten neck** by pulling the head tightly down to the shoulders...hold...let go...relax.

13. Tighten the **throat**, stretching the neck...hold...let go...relax.

14. Clench **jaw**...hold...let go...relax.

15. Purse **lips**...hold...let go...relax.

16. Clench **cheeks**...hold...let go...relax.

17. Tense the base of the **tongue** (in your throat) tightly...hold...let go...relax.

18. Tense the rest of the **tongue** (in your mouth)...hold...let go...relax.

19. Wrinkle **forehead.**...hold...let go...relax.

20. Squint your **eyes**...hold...let go...relax.

21. Make a face using all **facial muscles**...hold...let go...relax.

22. In a state of perfect relaxation, you should feel unwilling to move a single muscle in your body. Now continue relaxing, and when you wish to get up, count backward from four to one. You should then feel rested and refreshed, wide-awake and calm.

Like the resting breath, if you do this exercise regularly, in time you will be able to relax a specific muscle group very easily without as much concentration.

This is the end of our section on relaxation, but by no means is it the end of our talk of it. For more helpful exercises, see Appendix B. Remember, relaxation is not only the foundation of healthy, joyful singing; it is a part of the walls, the roof, the furniture and everything in between.

If you take the time to integrate any of these exercises into your daily life, you will not only increase your bodies' ability to function fluidly, increase your brain's ability to function more clearly, and therefore sing more easily, you will feel great too! So rest, relax and play!

1. Susan Colla is a vocal coach and instructor in the Los Angeles area.

2. Two methods of childbirth preparation teach this type of breathing: The Bradley Method, and the Grantly Dick-Reed Method.

3. Initially cited by Dr. Maxwell Maltz, in *Psychocybernetics,* Simon and Schuster, 1960.

4. Dr. Robert Anderson MD, now retired, formerly in Family Practice in Edmonds, Washington.

5. Adapted from a paper presented by Alan G. Hedberg, Ph.D., Fresno California

The voice is as individual as the snowflake. I hold each voice gently, never to crush the naturalness; yet firmly, to awaken the trueness.
- Kimberly Hadsell Chapron[1]

Chapter 5

Thinking and Believing

Disable the Fear

As Joan began to understand why singing was so difficult for her, I began an exercise. I sang a simple sound on one pitch, for about one second. It was a pitch I had already heard Joan sing, so I knew she could do it.

I asked Joan then to copy the sound I made as closely as she could. After some struggle and false starts, her fearful response was a sound of almost the same duration as mine, but with no association to the pitch.

It was emotionally excruciating for her to even make that sound. I could sense her throat close in on the tone, actually destroying her ability to keep a sound going. Her tightening throat also caused the pitch to contort and then cut off.

Joan reflected deep sadness and embarrassment as she heard the sound she made. It was easy to see she could hear the contrast between my sound and hers. Every time she attempted to sing, her heart broke anew.

"What are you feeling, Joan?" I asked

She replied, "I am so ashamed of the awful sounds I make when I try to sing…I guess I feel a lot of fear."

"Do you know what you're afraid of?" I queried.

After some thought, she said, "Well, I don't really know!"

I then suggested, "Could part of it be you are afraid that this precious part of you will be ridiculed and rejected?"

"Oh, yes! I feel like I am still a little girl, wanting so much for someone to accept my singing, because it is so precious to me. I think I am afraid I will make someone angry by my singing!"

Joan and I took more time to talk about and understand her feelings. I then asked, "What are the messages you are hearing that are attached to those feelings?"

It took some time for Joan to respond. Finally in a broken voice she said: " I guess I hear that all of my singing is just noise, that it is ugly and offensive to others' ears."

"Joan, I have some very important questions for you: Do you think your mom wanted you to feel this way about your singing voice? Did she intend to communicate to you that your voice was ugly and offensive to others? What do you think?"

"Well, I am sure she didn't have any intention of describing my singing voice! She was probably only thinking of the pressures she was under at the time."

I then queried, "Can you tell yourself the truth about your mother's comment, that she wasn't speaking at all about the sound of your voice, but instead was only needing quiet?"

"Why, yes! That makes sense! I never thought of it that way!" Joan's face reflected both relief and hope as she spoke. She chuckled with joy at the new understanding.

I continued, "Joan, it is very important that you tell yourself the truth about your voice. You have had a message inside you repeating over and over for 57 years. That message was based on a mistaken conclusion of a five year old."

Positive Self-Talk

"Whatever information our brain repeatedly hears, it believes and then acts upon. This is especially true if a belief is based on an incident connected to deep emotion. In order for your body to cooperate and allow your voice to grow freely, the negative lies that have dominated your brain must be erased," I told Joan.

"New, true and affirming messages must reprogram the way we think about our singing voices. The lies that have immobilized our musical growth for so many years must be recognized for what they are and replaced with positive, motivating, affirming thoughts."

These were new thoughts to Joan, and I could see clearly that it was uncomfortable for her to even begin to think of any positive response. I challenged, "Could you say truthfully that you have been given all you need to sing for joy?"

"Well, yes, I know intellectually that is true, but it's going to take a while to really believe it."

These thoughts—these lies—had become so ingrained in Joan's psyche that they sat squarely in the way of any of her efforts to sing. So, I asked, "Can you tell me some of the lies that have influenced your attitude toward your singing?"

"Well, one would definitely be, 'My singing voice is ugly noise.'" She added, "Also, 'I am not able to sing,'

"I have so many thoughts about my voice that I can see now are not true! I am amazed! After more thought she said, "Other lies would be, 'I do not have the equipment needed to sing' and 'I am stupid when it comes to music.'"

Though it was painful for Joan to say these things, each time she recognized the false beliefs she had lived with for so long, she felt a little freer. She was beginning to get a good idea of the way her thoughts had affected her voice.

Joan's primary problem—of most people struggling with singing—was one of fear, and if not fear then at least anxiety. Both of these are negative emotions that can lead to tensing muscles, due to our tendency to go into "fight or flight" when experiencing negative emotions.

Along with the fight or flight response, our desire to sing is so strong, and seems so unreachable, we work even harder. This is why many "non-singer's" voices may not sound pleasing. Again, we see how the vocal sound is distorted by tension.

A Story

I then told Joan a story. It's a true story that a wise man[2] told me during an exceptionally difficult time in my twenties:

My friend was in a people-helping profession and described being at a conference in a hotel in Washington state. Any conference that draws a group of males usually attracts a few female prostitutes.

Feeling compassion for these women, and understanding some of the causes of their situation, he befriended one of them, who very much wanted to leave that way of life. She had a daughter of whom she had lost custody, and had tried many times to break free of her destructive lifestyle, but her attempts always resulted in humiliation and failure.

This wise man knew that she was only fulfilling the script that she believed about herself. He knew that the only way out was to change the way she thought about herself. He said, "How much do you want to change the way you are living and thinking?"

"I would give anything" she fervently exclaimed, "to be able to get out of this horrible life that I am in!"

"Well, are you ready for a 'crash-course' in changing the way you think about yourself?"

"Absolutely!" she cried. "Please help me!"

"I am going to give you a list of positive statements that I see are true about you. You are to read them clearly and out loud, in front of a mirror if possible."

"If you want this bad enough, do this every hour on the hour, every day without fail. The statements are truths that may be very difficult for you to say, let alone believe. I am asking you to say them confidently, whether you believe them, or not."

He gave her the list:

> "I am beautiful.
>
> I am intelligent.
>
> I am capable.
>
> I have the ability to succeed in a respected career.
>
> I will be a good mother"

"Your subconscious mind is a computer," he told her. "It records information, stores it and makes it available for recall. Right now your subconscious is full of negative information; information that is not true, but needless to say, it is overwhelming."

"Everything that your senses have ever touched, tasted, seen, smelled, or heard is recorded in the computer. You have experienced a lot of negative in your life. You have

Chapter 5: Thinking and Believing

received and believed many, many lies about who you are and what you are capable of.

"This tremendous amount of negative recorded in your minds' computer has a great impact on your view of yourself and the choices you make, and even your bodies physical responses. When negative information or a memory surfaces, as you dwell on it, the negative thoughts multiply.

"It would be nice if we could just delete the entire contents of the computer and scrub it clean, but that is not possible. We would lose all of our positive memories and thoughts also.

"However, what we can do is begin to dilute the lies, little by little, with truth. In time, and with practice, the positive truth can become more dominant than the negative lies and actually free us to begin to live them out.

"The process of diluting the lies will take some time. If you take a clear glass and put a small amount of dark liquid, as you add clear liquid into the glass the dark liquid will gradually, though it is still present, become undetectable. Are you ready to do some intense work?"

"Absolutely!" she exclaimed.

A few days later, he got a frantic call from her. "I've been doing what you told me," she said, "but now I'm breaking out in hives, all over my body—I don't understand! What's happening?"

"You're telling your mind, body and soul things that that they haven't heard in years, and your body doesn't know how to react to it," he explained. "Just keep it up."

She did keep it up, and within a week the hives began to go away, and it became easier and easier to make the affirmations with confidence. She was able to leave behind her life of prostitution and regained custody of her daughter. She eventually got a real estate license and became a successful real estate agent.

By rebuilding the destructive thought-patterns into positive affirmations, and diluting the information in her subconscious, she was able to let go of the destructive life choices and begin to fulfill her potential.

Lose the Lies

The body believes what the mind thinks, so if you are repeatedly telling yourself that you can't sing, chances are good that you won't. You'll have to determine for yourself what those lies are, but following are a few that may have been rolling around inside your head. You may come up with something different.

Lie #1: If my voice doesn't sound like a performer's, I shouldn't sing at all.

This is patently untrue, for a number of reasons, some already discussed. To begin, as I've already mentioned, most recording artists' voices are altered by dubbing and digital syntheses. What you hear on a CD or the radio is not reality.

Keep in mind that even those who sing well without electronic enhancement have been training their voices for years, while you—especially if your musical development has been slowed or stopped—quite simply have not. But remember, it's never too late!

We don't discourage people from running simply because they're not Michael Johnson, or from cooking because they aren't Wolfgang Puck. So, why do we discourage people from singing just because they aren't professional performers?

Lie #2: There are good voices, and there are bad voices—and mine is bad

There are no such things as "good" voices or "bad" voices, any more than there are good or bad fingerprints, or good or bad snowflakes. Each person has an individual, unique voice, and none is any better or worse than any other. They are simply different.

Plenty of people with what our society may call "bad voices" have gone on to be very successful performers—Joe Cocker, Louie Armstrong and Bob Dylan, to name a few.

Lie #3: I've heard my voice recorded, and it's terrible!

This is untrue for a few of the reasons detailed above—you may be comparing it to something unrealistic, you're voice hasn't been trained at all, etc.—as well as some others.

Most recording devices we would hear our voices on have only a fraction of the sensitivity and response to the many overtones and textures that make up a singing voice. Again, we are used to hearing voices that are produced on very expensive, high tech equipment. Comparing a "home-made" recording of your voice with that of a professional recording is like comparing an apple with grandma's apple pie.

However, even I have to admit, though I have been singing semi-professionally for 30 years, and have been teaching voice for the same, only in the last few years have I been able to enjoy listening to my voice on a recording.

Why has this taken so long for me? I believe that my own personal maturing process and self-acceptance has finally brought me to a place of strength. I can now "own" my voice without being hypercritical.

You may find this a factor in your view of your voice. It may be that however beautiful your voice, you will only hear the flaws. This is another illustration of the importance of practicing positive self-talk, to both know and believe what is true about yourself and your singing voice.

Lie #4: People who know what they are taking about have told me I have a bad voice.

The simple fact is that if someone has told you that you have a bad voice, this person doesn't know what he or she is talking about! Likely, they have said these things out of ignorance, because they don't actually know anything about the singing voice.

If they do know a good deal about music, then they are coming out of the destructive musical mentality that has been so pervasive in the last century. Trust me, as someone who does know what she is talking about, there is no such thing as a "bad" voice. Every voice has unique qualities that distinguish it from others.

What some might label as a "bad voice" is usually a combination of issues. The most frequent issues are lack of tonal nurturing in childhood and the emotional roadblocks that can result. But, these are both problems that can be overcome.

Lie #5: The only reason for singing is to perform for others.

This is possibly the most insidious lie of all. As music developed through time, it was most certainly not developed for performance! It was a way to pass down stories, to bring together a community, to worship, to mourn - not to put on a show. The purpose of singing is first personal expression, not performance.

Lie #6: If I am having fun, I can't be making good music.

As we have already seen, our musical abilities grow in a context of play and experimentation. Play is appropriate and a valid path to musical growth.

However, as a young child is always listening and evaluating his interactions with the sounds he is experiencing, our play must be in the context of developing our musical ear. Learning musical skills cannot be separated from musical hearing. So, play – but first, second, and last, include your "musical ear" in that play.

Affirming the Truth

Once you have identified some of the lies that have been holding you back, it is time to make a decision to stop thinking and believing them. To eliminate the negative, destructive thoughts you must not only refuse to dwell on the negative, but also replace them with affirming truths about yourself and about your voice.

Practice Opportunity #4: "Affirmations"

Because the human voice is such a deep and integral part of our whole being, some important affirmations may not deal strictly with just your singing voice. I encourage you to ask a friend to help you come up with a list of affirmations that fit you personally.

Following is a list of some suggestions to start with:

- *I have value.*
- *I am capable.*
- *I have everything I need to sing and enjoy it.*
- *By practicing the basics, I can begin to enjoy singing.*
- *I am intelligent enough to learn how to use my musical ear.*
- *With practice, I will find the singing voice I was meant to have.*
- *My simple, plain singing voice is beautiful.*

- *My singing voice is uniquely special. No one else has a voice with the unique beauty of mine.*

- *People who say my singing voice is "bad" don't know what they are talking about or have a very unrealistic and distorted idea about singing.*

The key to using these affirmations is repetition. Perhaps, like the woman in the story, you are motivated to repeat them to yourself in the mirror, every hour on the hour. Perhaps you aren't able to do it so often. Perhaps you can't bring yourself to say them in front of a mirror—for years, I couldn't.

But, however often you do it, do it regularly and repeat them often. And remember that this is a process, not something that you do and then quit, because you're suddenly "fixed." Incorporating affirming truth into our psyche is an ongoing process of renewing our minds.

We cannot separate these mental and emotional aspects of ourselves from the physical act of singing. Therefore, this process of understanding the lies about our voices, and replacing them with self-nurturing truths is an integral part of learning to sing.

Once you are moving forward in setting this solid foundation, your road to singing growth and confidence will be much smoother. You are ready to begin developing the physiological and brain functions that are needed to sing for joy. As we begin to feel better about our "equipment" and potential, we can begin to experiment and play!

---

1. www.womeninproduction.com

2. David Bury is the Chief Operating Officer of Hopes Gift International; He has served as Executive Director of Youth for Christ in Seattle, Portland, and Los Angeles (San Gabriel and Inland Valley chapter).

Your music is the key...play it and you will find the door...to yourself.
- Donna Harrington

Chapter 6

Finding My Musical Ear

Straight Pitching

The number one complaint that I get from "non-singers" is that they can't sing "on key"—that they are "tone deaf." The number one desire I hear from non-singers is to be able to confidently sing on pitch.

It certainly was Joan's desire. She had a limited range, but she very much wanted to be able to sing Christmas carols with the rest of her church.

This, however, was difficult to do when she couldn't hit the notes. She didn't understand why something that seemed so easy for so many people was so difficult for her. It wasn't that much of a mystery, though. Since childhood, she had not used the part of her brain that deals with pitch in music, or developed her musical ear.

Our first task was to consciously begin to use the tonal portion of the brain. I asked Joan to listen to some spoken words, just as I had said them.

The tones that give our everyday speech meaning and expressiveness are actual musical pitches. The fact that we can speak with socially acceptable tonal inflections proves that we are <u>not</u> tone deaf.

Our expressive speaking voice utilizes the same tonal center of the brain that we use in music. However, with arrested musical development, a strong wall can drop between the simple spoken patterns and the singing pitches.

Therefore, we begin with the familiar, the safe, and gradually transition to the "strange world" of the singing voice and the musical ear.

Practice Opportunity #5: "Spoken Intonation"

1. *Expressively say the word "hello."*
2. *Break it up into its two syllables and emphasize each one of their pitches strongly:* 'HEL LO' *(This visualization is only an example of what your expression could be.)*
3. *Say this, again emphasizing each pitch, but hold each syllable for a longer time.*
4. *Spend a few minutes repeating this exercise, increasing the time that you hold each syllable.*
5. *Repeat this exercise with any expressive words you choose.*
6. *Relax and say the 'hello' again, this time using different patterns of pitches by speaking with a variety of expressive meanings: happy, fearful, jokingly, angry, romantic, etc.*

Eventually, two things will happen. First, you will almost undoubtedly realize that you are singing. Second, you will either be comfortable with this, or you will hit a wall and tense up. If the latter happens, don't worry about it, as this can be a normal response when we begin to connect with the singing voice.

What you do need to recognize is that you have unintentionally built this wall between singing and speaking and it does not need to be there. This wall actually exists in your "musical ear." It is in the area of this "musical ear" that our musical play must take place.

The only difference between the pitches we use in speaking and those that we use in singing is the variety. We still use the same vocal cords and—more importantly—we use the same part of the brain to hit pitches in spoken intonation as we do to hit pitches when we sing.

Activating Audiation

This leads us to something else that many people do not realize about singing—we *don't* sing with our vocal cords. Though the actual sound is made in the vocal cords, our conscious effort is actually centered in the brain. We sing with our ears and our brains, not our vocal cords. This is our musical ear.

There are no brains in our vocal cords that we can control them with, and we cannot consciously make our vocal cords find any pitches. The problem that many people have when they attempt to sing is that they attempt to find the pitches by manhandling their vocal cords, when what they need to do is think about the sound and let the brain do the work.

What actually happens is the brain sends the correct signals to the nerves in the vocal cords. Whatever is thought or "heard" in the brain is automatically sung by the vocal cords. Hearing and discriminating pitches in the brain is how we use our musical ear. Another label for this is "audiation."[2]

Practice Opportunity #6: "Beginning Audiation"

To activate audiation means that we begin to intentionally use the tonal thinking part of our brain (our musical ear).

1. *Sit quietly and begin to become aware of the many sounds around you. You may hear the refrigerator humming, the fan on your computer, a clock ticking, cars driving by, birds singing, the radio, anything!*

2. *Replay these sounds one by one in your mind.*

3. *Now think of familiar sounds that you are not presently hearing: your car shifting gears, a hair blower, the phone ringing, the vacuum cleaner, someone typing on the computer, a familiar persons' greeting, etc.*

The part of the brain that you are using to do this is the same part a singer uses to remember and sing a song! To be able to sing using the musical ear there is a simple formula:

      Step 1: Hear a sound

      Step 2: Think the sound (audiate)

      Step 3: Sing the sound

These basic steps are critical to learning to sing on pitch. Our "musical brain" is where musical sound is interacted with and perceived. The ear is only a conduit to the brain. The most important and most difficult work in learning how to sing is developing an easy access to our musical brain, and being able to interact with it. This critical piece of the brain where music both is created and perceived is standard equipment with every functioning human brain, and can be developed.

I have found that those who struggle with pitch have been skipping the "thinking" stage (Step 2) in attempts to sing. They, when not understanding Step 2, try to find that sound with the voice without using their musical ear.

By and skipping over the critical "audiating" step, the tuneful singing process becomes very complex and almost impossible. The key to confident singing is to let the brain hear the sound first and then the connections with production in the vocal cords are automatic.

This portion of your brain may be a little rusty at first when it comes to singing, but remember, if you speak with socially acceptable inflection, then you already using the equipment you need. Repeating this exercise can help shake off the dust and begin to develop a healthy, working musical ear.

Practice Opportunity #7: "Audiating Intonation"

Remember the "Spoken Intonation" exercise above? Now you are ready to take it to a new step.

1. *Sit quiet and think about the different words you used, beginning with "hello." Think that first "hello" in your memory.*

2. *Repeat it several times, first in your thoughts, and then out loud.*

3. *Now think of the various different expressive ways you said the hello. Focus on one at a time, and repeat it in your mind several times.*

4. *Can you go back to a previous "hello" and remember how it sounded?*

By doing this exercise, you are building "catalogs" of sound patterns in your brain, developing your musical ear. It is the same process needed to learn the musical patterns we need to be able to sing. So begin to exercise your audiating skills as often as possible.

To continue:

5. *Think of the song "Row, Row, Row Your Boat." Can you hear the melody in your brain? Can you hear the melody without the words? You are audiating!*

Congratulations!

6. *Now sing the "Row, Row..." out loud <u>as you continue to hear it in your brain</u>. You have now taken audiation to another level! By hearing the sounds in our heads as we sing, we can sing in tune.*

7. *Think of a favorite song you heard recently on the radio or a CD. How much of it can you sing in your mind? Keep going and don't give up. I'll bet your brain can do more than you think it can!*

8. *Now quietly hum a small piece of the same song out loud. Try not to copy the style or the quality of the singer's voice. Instead think the pitches, and then sing the pitches.*

Absorb and Experiment

Joan had been a preschool teacher for many years and was also a loving grandmother. She loved to get down and interact with children on their level. I think that is one reason she was able to focus on these skills—she was willing to lose her inhibitions and become like a little child who is hungry to learn new skills of expression.

Through thirty years of research on how children learn music, Dr. Edwin Gordon has both concluded and proven that children learn basic musical skills in the same way they learn speaking skills.[3]

A child first listens to and absorbs the sounds around them, and then gradually begins to experiment with making his own sounds.[4] Through this listening and experimentation, a child is building a vocabulary of sounds that will be with him for the rest of his life.

In the same way, we all have been building catalogs of sounds in our brains from our birth. As I see it, the problems arise as we begin to experiment with those sounds and receive either negative feedback or no feedback at all. This is true, I believe, if we are six months or sixty years old.

If those who nurture a child have a negative understanding of their own musical ability, that child will incorporate the same view as normal for himself as well. Our attitude toward our environment can be learned from others, just as our musical growth can be slowed or shut down because of a lack of positive musical nurture.

As adults, though, we have the ability to create much of our own environment, and so we are able to create an atmosphere where we can be nurtured musically. It is greatly to our advantage if there are children around, because we can join in with their musical growth.

Imitate and Assimilate

In the next stage[5] a child begins attempts to imitate some of the sounds he is hearing. As this stage progresses, the child realizes that his efforts are not the same as what he is hearing. A child in a nurturing environment will continue to attempt to imitate the sounds heard more closely.

As adults learning to audiate, we can use the same principles a child uses naturally. Here we see the value of the simple imitation that we have already applied in the above exercises. Find some young children, get down on their level and play echo games. If they can't imitate you, you imitate them. You will grow and they will grow.

Children also will often make up their own improvised songs, singing whatever words come into their head to whatever pitches are a part of the catalogs they have been developing in their brains. This is also a good practice exercise that will help you sharpen your musical ear.

To give you some tools to begin to "play" with your singing voice, there is a simple tonal pattern that may be the first melody learned around the world.[7] In the United States it is a taunting song such as "you can't catch me," while in Indonesia it is the tune for a hide-and-seek game—

"Nya, nya,   nya, nya –

     nya,   nya – "

Nya, nya, nya, nya, nya, nya

Practice Opportunity #8: "Nya, Nya Play-Song"

1. *Audiate the "play-song" in your thoughts. Imagine some of the fun you may have had as a child with this little pattern.*

2. *Sing the pattern in the context of the play you remember as a child (though the*

mocking attitude is not necessary). By audiating and then singing it, you will be developing your musical ear, as well as your ability to sing.

The key to developing a "musical ear" is practice—and lots of it.[6] Relaxed, uninhibited repetition is the only way to develop an undeveloped "musical ear." So, play these games often, replay sounds in your head all the time, and echo noises whenever you get the chance.

I find that many who are recovering from some stage of "tonal shutdown" actually have an extremely sensitive ear for pitch. It appears that without guidance or affirmation, when they have heard the small inconsistencies in pitch as they sing –ones that those with a less sensitive ear may not pick up– they assume they do not have the correct pitch. Eventually they can unconsciously shutdown their musical ear, hiding their singing voice.

Once these individuals realize that they have a great ear, their next task is to learn to trust their ear, along with thinking pitches before they are sung. Their sensitive ear becomes a great gift, once they begin to trust it.

Soon you will discover that you are able to hear things in you head—and repeat them—much better than you ever could before. From there, it's not too far to begin hearing a note *before* you sing it, thinking it, and then singing it—with confidence, because you've already audiated.

1. Throughout this book, I am illustrating the movement of sounds by placing syllables higher or lower on the page, demonstrating how high or low a sound is in relation to the sounds that come both before and after. In this particular illustration, "lo" would sound lower than "hel."

2. Dr. Edwin Gordon defines audiation as assimilating and comprehending music that we have heard; *Learning Sequences in Music*, GIA Publications, Chicago, c.1997, p. 4

3. Gordon, Edwin. *A Music Learning Theory for Newborn and Young Children,* GIA Publications, Chicago. c.1997, p. 5

4. Valario, Reynolds, Bolton, Taggart and Gordon. *Music Play.* GIA Publications, Chicago, c.1998, p 8.

5. According to Dr. Gordon, Imitation is the ability to discern the sameness or difference between what one is singing and what is heard, and reproduce the sound with some precision. *Music Learning Theory for Newborn and Young Children,* GIA Publications, Chicago. c.1997. p.35.

6. Dr. Gordon states: "Audiation is not acquired immediately or quickly. We acquire skill in audiation through a sequential process over time..." *A Music Learning Theory for Newborn and Young Children,* GIA Publications, Chicago. c.1997. p.19.

7. I have done informal research by interviewing individuals native to various parts of Asia, Europe, Africa, and the Americas. All that I have spoken with have learned the same simple tonal pattern in their earliest years as "play songs."

Remember... You don't HAVE to practice! You GET to practice!
- David Mount[1]

Chapter 7

Moving Into New Rooms

The Value of Understanding

Another roadblock that people on the road to joyful singing experience all too often is simply a lack of knowledge about their voice. This is understandable—if you have been afraid to use your voice for anything but speaking, how would you know what other possibilities there are?

Begin to explore your voice. Again, this brings us back to the theme of dropping our inhibitions and thinking like a little child. Spend time experimenting with the many different sounds that you can make with your voice, from the very high to the very low, from the very soft to the very loud, from the normal to the just plain ridiculous. (However, be careful not to cause any discomfort to your voice or throat.)

As you experiment, you may discover a fact that many people do not realize, but one that is crucial to effective singing: we appear to have at least two different voices. That is to say, we have separate resonating chambers, or "rooms."

Just as a violin or acoustical guitar string would not sound like much if it were not connected to the body of the instrument, our voice would be barely audible if it were not for the resonating cavities that allow the sound vibrations to amplify and enrich.

In each of these "rooms" we can feel the sounds vibrating as we move our voice up or down. When our voice is sounding lower the sounds center their resonating around the collarbone, throat, and up into the mouth. As the voice moves higher and the body is relaxed, the vibrating sensations move up into the roof of the mouth, the sinuses, and even the forehead and skull.

For simplicity's sake, we will focus on the two major resonation "rooms," (sometimes called "registers") the head, and the chest. The chest voice is lower, and is the one we generally use to speak, so it is familiar to us. It uses the deeper lower sounds and its vibrations can be felt primarily in the upper chest throat and lower jaw.

The lower or "chest-voice" is visceral, and connects deeply to our simpler emotions. It is sometimes thought of as "sensuous" and because this part of our voice is not present in most children's voices, we may identify it as our "adult" voice, and assume that the higher voice is only a remnant of childhood.

Finding Your Head

The higher "head" voice can feel very different from the lower range of the voice. I find that many students don't even realize that this is a usable part of their voice, and because of lack of use, they are very uncomfortable exploring it. The sensations are foreign, and a combination of a lack of confidence and unfamiliarity can cause avoidance of these strange sounds and sensations.

As students discover the higher portion of the voice, they realize it is a piece they have been aware of, but have never associated with the singing voice. Some students, with a flash of realization say: "Oh, you mean my 'baby-voice'", "'Barbie doll voice'" or "'Mickey Mouse voice'" etc.

Our head voice is what we use when we quietly exclaim in a positive manner, such as finally understanding the punch line of a joke, the "Ah-ha!" that comes with great satisfaction or realization. The natural head voice is very simple and child-like. It does not need effort in the throat, just energy from the diaphragm and an open mouth.

Of Birds and Cows

When I am teaching children to use their entire voices, I use a cow puppet to identify the lower part of the voice. I encourage them experience the rich, deep vibrations of a resonant "moooo" and talk about the deep round sounds they are experiencing. (At the same time, I make sure they understand when they begin to become adults, their voices will be able to go even lower, especially for boys.)

With young children, I identify the head or higher voice with a bird puppet. We pretend we are birds, tweeting and flying around the room. I encourage each child to imagine the skinny, thin sounds up higher in their heads. I find that both children and adults are more comfortable using the chest voice, since they've generally never had an occasion to use the head voice, and use the chest voice all the time. Therefore using the head voice can feel silly at first.

Men will often complain that the head voice is their falsetto, that it isn't their real voice. The truth is, the "falsetto" is not "false," at all but is a genuine part of a man's voice, though it may be very weak from lack of use. Women generally don't have the same view of the head voice, but do typically complain that it hurts to use it. This, again, is because they are not used to using it and do not relax when they do.

Joan was having a very difficult time finding her head voice, and just wasn't comfortable with it at all. However, Joan was an avid Seattle Mariners fan, and together we discovered that Mariners radio announcer Dave Niehaus' trademark excited cry "my, oh my!" used the head voice. From that time on, whenever she struggled in finding that part of her voice, she just thought of the fun she had at Mariner games and exclaimed "My, oh my!" and she was back on track.

Practice Opportunity #9: "Moving Upstairs"

1. *Put your hand on your sternum, right in the middle of your chest, and hum as low as you can. You may feel the vibrations of the sounds in your upper chest. The more relaxed you are, the more likely you are to feel the reverberation in your sternum and collarbones.*

2. *Move your hands up and around your throat. Here, because this is the location of the larynx ("voice box") the vibrations are very easy to feel.*

3. *Gradually begin to slide your voice upward, making sure you are relaxed as you move, allowing the vibrations to move up into your upper mouth and head area. It is best not to force this to happen, but instead to **allow the vibrations to move.***

*Be sure to **let** your voice go high, and not to force it, both when you're doing this hum exercise and when you're singing. If you force the head voice, the sound will come out flat and strained.*

Singing in the natural head voice with good support from the diaphragm and a relaxed body, can be as effortless as a sigh.

Practice Opportunity #10: "The Contented Sigh"

1. *In a very relaxed state, release a light sigh of contentment. Feel the ease in the voice as you repeat this.*

2. *Continuing in a relaxed attitude, thinking in a positive manner and repeat the signs, moving them higher and higher in your voice. (If any sensation of strain occurs, move lower, focus on relaxing and gradually, positively move up.)*

3. *Begin a sigh but instead of letting the pitch fall, allow it to stay at the same pitch level, continuing the relaxed, effortless attitude.*

This sigh, remaining on a sustained pitch, is your pure, natural head voice. It results from a freedom and positive mindset that actually opens up our resonators in the higher range.

The "positive mindset" I am referring to is an extremely important segment of our singing voice. Most voice teachers call it the "inside smile." I like to label it as the "inside 'yes!'" because it is less a smile than an attitude of the mind.

It is amazing to see that an inner joy actually creates a more flexible, clear, resilient singing voice. When the songwriter in the Psalms wrote, "sing for joy," he was giving a key for fulfilling and successful singing!

Practice Opportunity #11: "The Crow"

1. *Relax your throat and think of the delicious freedom a bird might have gliding through the sky. Retaining this positive thought, make several 'caw' sounds like a crow. (Yes, you will feel silly, but remember "as a child.")*

2. *Now take a relaxed breath and begin the "caw" high in your voice, gradually letting the pitch fall. Allow the vibrations to move down slowly continuing until a low relaxed rattle.*

The head voice is so important because it is the only healthy way to hit high notes. Many people who do not understand their head voice will attempt to hit high notes using only their chest voice, and this is both damaging and unpleasant sounding.

Gravity

It is interesting that the principle of gravity appears to apply to our singing voices. I see this when we begin to use the head voice. When we begin to move into the head voice by starting low and moving up (as in "Moving Upstairs," above) the voice has a much more difficult time of letting go of the stronger, more familiar low sounds and moving into the higher. Therefore, as we move up, we push the chest voice to its limits, and it can sound strained and distorted.

Over-singing using the lower chest voice and stretching it up into the higher range is known as "the belt," and it's ruined more voices on Broadway than anything else. It generally sounds strident and flat, and causes hoarseness, discomfort, and eventually can permanently damage the vocal chords.

When we begin making sounds in our higher, lighter head voice, we can begin much more easily by starting with a high relaxed sound and bringing that lightness down well into the chest voice area. This is how we blend the two registers into one unified voice.

Two Become One

From my experience, to blend these two "voices" into one flexible voice, building the higher vocal quality must be the focus of our efforts. Sounds should be initiated first in the head voice. As we then move down into the lower areas, we need to stay in the head voice as long as possible, without giving in to the lower voice.

At the same time, the lower voice must allow the higher quality to move into its "room." By consistently practicing this in both exercises and singing songs that start higher and move downward,[2] you will begin to see a unified voice emerge that does not have weak middle areas.

When a person first begins using their head voice, it can sound weak and breathy. This comes from a lack of use, and as you use it more often, it will grow stronger. These exercises can help build a good foundation. As you are building that foundation, you are gently and gradually allowing yourself to sing songs up in that register. Sing with freedom and joy, not afraid, but confident that you can!

1. David Mount has a teaching studio in Redlands, CA; *www.davidmount.com*

2. See Appendix C for a brief list of common songs that begin with descending melodies.

As long as you try, you will not fail.
- *Unknown*

Chapter 8

Critical Connections

Breath and Sound

You may be thinking that those high notes are not as easy as I have said. You would be right because we have still not covered a very important area that we need for easy singing. Do you remember when we discussed the breath earlier? Our breath gives us not only the release we need to sing, but also the energy and power behind the tone.

The breath is the tool that creates a singing sound. Though the actual pitch is created in the vocal cords (responding to nerve stimulus from the brain), our ability to hold out a note, or sing a melody is dependent on the breath.

What we must do is learn how to connect the breath to the tone of the voice. Below are some exercises that with help.

Practice Opportunity #12: "The Sssssnake"

(Do this exercise where you can see the second hand of a clock or watch. Or better yet, have someone read the instructions aloud to you, so you can concentrate on the physiological factors.)

1. *Review your deep resting breaths. Make sure you are fully relaxed, especially in the upper chest and throat.*

2. *When you are confident of your deep, resting breath and you are releasing any tension in the upper chest/ throat area, after a full deep breath, hold that breath.*

3. *Let the breath go as you create a "hissing" sound between the tongue and the teeth.*

   This "sssss" should be steady and even, not fluctuating. Pace your release of breath as you "hiss" so you can extend the length of the "hiss." The muscle you are using to control the steadiness and pacing of the breath is your diaphragm.

4. *Once you get a feel for pacing, but continuing to be relaxed, use the clock or watch to time the length you can continue a steady hiss without taking a breath.*

   A good goal is 25 seconds, but don't bring in tension as you try to lengthen your time. Any tension will sabotage your ability to extend a breath, so continue to focus on relaxation.

5. *As you exhale, quickly you will feel you are running out of air. However, instead of tensing the upper chest (which we do to attempt to empty the breath), focus on relaxing the upper chest.*

   At the same time, gently lift the diaphragm up toward the lungs. Picture yourself rolling up plastic bags from the bottom to get all of the air out. You will find you have a lot more air than you imagined.

   Do this exercise 5 times per day and you will be amazed to see your breath capacity and control grow!

Practice Opportunity #13: "The Jumping Ssssnake"

1. *Follow the exercise above, but do not focus on the length of the "hiss." Instead think "1, 2, 3, 1, 2, 3, etc. punching a strong pulse on every "3." It might look like this: ssSsssSssSsssS etc.*

2. *Now repeat on a new breath, but this time create the pulse on each "beat" possibly looking like this: S S S S S S S etc. (The underlines demonstrate when you push a burst of air out of your diaphragm. Make sure you are not clenching in the throat at the same time.)*

   After repeating this several times, you will notice your diaphragm is tired. This is good! You are building strength!

The same breath-energy that created the "hiss," is what the voice uses to sing. To make this connection, consonants are wonderful tools. Consonants, especially the percussive ones like "t," "p," "k," "f," and of course "s," can help us make this connection.

Chapter 8: Critical Connections

Practice Opportunity #14: "Percussive Power"

1. *Pretend that you are blowing out 1,000 candles on a huge birthday cake (Sometimes we feel we can really live that long!)*
2. *Now pretend to spit a watermelon seed across the room by putting diaphragm power behind a "tooo!"*
3. *Now create a high, strong sigh sound like "The Crow" but say: "Tah!" Repeat this several times, making sure your throat, shoulders, and chest are relaxed.*
4. *Sing any simple note patterns (i.e. "Three Blind Mice") using the "Tah" to begin each pitch. You may feel that your voice is out of control, cracking and doing all sorts of strange things, but this is normal.*

With this exercise you actually are beginning to fill your vocal resonators with the extra "punch" the diaphragm is giving the consonants. What you are hearing and feeling is the sound vibrating in your resonators.

The cracking may just be the result of using a new part of your voice that isn't yet under control. Don't be afraid of the sensations, and explore them. Just be aware of not pushing these sounds to the point that you are experiencing any discomfort.

5. *Sing a song with words and try to sing each consonant with the energy from your diaphragm. It may not sound all that great at first, but as you continue to apply the principle, you will find it much easier to fill your resonators, and also to have a strong, relaxed voice on the higher sounds.*

Mouth and Sound

The mouth is one of the major resonators for our singing voice. However, most of us don't take full advantage of this space because we don't open our mouths any more that we would for normal conversation. The first step in learning how to use our mouths in singing is to learn how to open our mouths without creating tension.

Practice Opportunity #15: "Open Up"

1. *Place your hands on each side of your face directly in front of the ears. The index-finger tips should be resting on the piece of cartilage that would cover the ear canal*

if pressed.

2. *Gently massage the entire area around the back of the jaw (just in front of the ears). If your fingers find any tender spots, gently massage those with a little more pressure.*

3. *Press your fingertips deeply into the face area just above where your back molars meet.*

4. *While maintaining pressure with the fingertips, draw them down, gently causing your lower jaw to drop from the back.*

Most of us think of our jaws as opening by swinging down in the front. However, the Temporo-Mandibular joint of the jaw is not a "hinge" but is rather a "floating joint."

This means that when the entire lower jaw is relaxed, it drops down from the back at the same time as the front. This is a natural occurrence when we yawn. However, again, just like the difficulty with the resting breath, when most of us open our mouths, we drop from the front, which creates more tension in the entire mouth.

5. *Practice dropping the jaw from the back several times. Say "yah" as you open, letting the jaw drop loosely. This feels a little strange, and if we weren't looking in a mirror, we might think we looked like a "zombie."*

6. *Now sing a repeated "yah, yah, yah" while dropping the jaw from the back again on each new "yah." Nothing should be forced, but instead allow the jaw to drop open.*

In our culture, we carry a tremendous amount of tension in our jaws. A large percentage of my adult and teen students over the years have "catches" or "popping" in their jaws when they open.

However, if we open in the manner outlined above, the entire mouth area is relaxed, the jaw can drop farther, and the "catches" or "popping" (possibly a symptom of scar tissue from TMJ Syndrome) may be eliminated.

To continue:

7. *As you continue to practice opening, check the size of your mouth's opening by*

*placing your first two fingers **vertically** between the teeth. If there is not enough room for both fingers then, work more on relaxing your jaw with the massage to allow it to open. This may feel uncomfortably wide at first, but as you look in the mirror, you can see it looks fine.*

Song Without Words

I usually don't start students singing words right away, because our "American-eeze" language is not very "singable." In fact, our American version of English is very difficult to sing. But don't get discouraged! There are some simple tricks that make all the difference.

The most singable language in the world is said to be Italian. There has been speculation that the Italian language was sung first before it was spoken (but I think that speculation had a tongue in the cheek!). The first thing that makes Italian so singable is that there are no "diphthongs" like we have in English.

A diphthong is a combination of vowel sounds with no consonants dividing them. For example, the word "feel" has both an "eee" sound and "ih" sound. If we sing "feel" as we speak it, the sound quality of our voice as we sing (not pitch, but the character of the voice) would vary greatly with the changing vowel sounds, because the sound is sustained or "held out." It would probably look like this written out: "feeeeeeeiiiiiiiillllllll." Not a pretty sound, is it?

The trick that singers learn from Italian is to sing only one vowel sound per word. In English, we usually sing and maintain the first vowel sound until moving to the next note or syllable. To sing the word "feel," we would hold on to the "eee" sound and only put on the "ih" sound as we finished the word with the "l."

Practice Opportunity #16: "Pure Vowels"

1. *Say "mah." Now sing "mah" on one long tone. Listen carefully to the "ah" sound. Does the sound change at all or do you hear just one pure "ah"?*
2. *Look in a mirror and sing the "ah" this time as you slowly open or close your mouth while you are singing. Do you hear the subtle changes in the sound of your voice as you move your jaw? To produce a consistent **vocal** sound, we need to produce a*

*consistent **vowel** sound.*

3. *Say "mah" as you would say "Mom" but without the "uhm" ending. (The vowel is an "ah" sound even though the word has an "o.") Your jaw should be dropping open to at least the "two-finger" distance.*

4. *Now sing "mah, mah, mah, mah" while looking in the mirror. Is your jaw dropping consistently? Are you maintaining one even vowel sound?*

    If not, continue to work with relaxation and careful listening. As we drop the jaw, it should immediately go to the open, relaxed position with which the entire "ah" will be voiced. Any moving of the jaw while singing the vowel sound will distort the sound.

5. *Continue to practice the "mah" on different pitches, working for the same, pure, simple vowel sound.*

6. *Apply this same principle of pure vowel sounds to the various vowels we use in "American-eeze." (A, E, I, O, U) using both long and short sounds.*

    You may find that you cannot open the "E" as wide as the other's. That is normal. Just be sure your jaw is not jutting forward or rigid.

7. *Now choose a simple song that you enjoy then slowly and quietly sing the song while looking into a mirror. Open your mouth comfortably on each word, listening and watching for pure vowels.*

Can you hear a different voice when you open and use the pure sounds? Continue to train your ear to not only hear the pitches, but also hear clear, simple vowel sounds. To master these skills takes time, and while understand you are just getting started you can begin to grow a voice you are not ashamed of.

Begin to listen to singers that you admire. Listen to the way they pronounce vowels and consonants. Learn from a variety of individuals, but don't try to copy their actual singing. Just apply these principles to your own unique voice, and play!

Anything worth doing takes time and effort.
- unknown

Chapter 9

Sneaky Tricks

Note: The contents of this chapter focus on technical aspects of performance singing. It may be confusing, but don't be discouraged. In fact, to sing for your own enjoyment, these techniques are not important. If you find yourself frustrated, but would like to grow in these skills, find a friend who has had some vocal training, or a teacher with whom you feel comfortable.

There's More?

You may be thinking by now, "Hey, this is too much! I can't remember all of this! All I want to do is to sing for fun!"

Good for you! If you want to sing for your own enjoyment, then do it, and don't worry about how you sound. By covering these more technical issues, I am hoping you will understand why your voice may sound the way it does.

Do you still want more? Great! Here are some more "tricks of the trade."

The "R"

Sing and hold out the word "word." Not easy is it? Our "American-eeze" "R" is not easily singable. Try to sing just the letter "R" alone. Ouch! Not too pleasant is it?

There are sneaky ways to get around singing the unsingable "R." The simplest way is to eliminate it altogether. For instance, when singing "word," instead sing "wuhd."

If this sounds too stilted for you, sneak in a little 'r' with the tongue only, not the lips. Experiment some with the "American-eeze" "R" to find what your tongue actually does. At first, you may have to hold your hand over your lips so they don't move, but you'll get the idea.

The "L"

Say the word "fill." Now, sing "fill." Strange isn't it? Just what do we do with the "L?" As you have probably already realized, our "American-eeze" "L" is another unsingable consonant when it appears in the middle or the end of a word.

The secret here is not to pronounce the "L" until the beginning of the next syllable or word. Then, as we move on, we slip in a quick "L" with only the tip of the tongue. It's sneaky, but it works!

The Worst "World"

If you thought the L's and R's were tough, try putting them together and adding a D. This happens in a few words that seem to appear in songs a lot. Sing "world" holding it out for a few seconds. Before you dissolve in fits of laughter or tears, just try eliminating the "R," use only the tip of the tongue on the "L" and end with a resounding "D." You did it! Now that wasn't so hard was it?

Think Before You Sing

I find there is a simple habit that many have which can cause a voice to sound like it is going out of tune, or actually pull it out of tune when we start the first sounds of a sung word with our speaking voice. Sing the word "mom." Listen carefully as you sing. Did the "m" start on a lower pitch than the note you sang?

These "spoken starts" is a habit that can be broken. By focusing on the pitch before you sing, instead of the word, in time you can break that nasty habit. It takes concentration, but you can do it with practice. Do you remember the song you sang in front of the mirror working on pure vowel sounds? Sing the same song, but this time listen carefully for the way you begin each word. As you tune your ear to hear the "spoken starts," you will quickly begin to eliminate them.

Give Up the Glottal

Beginning to sing a word that begins with a vowel can be tricky if you are the kind of person who puts a lot of intensity into our singing. It seems, many musical phrases start with either the personal pronoun "I," an "E" as in "every" or "A" as in "all." Each of these sounds when spoken, begin with quick, gentle pinching of the vocal folds.

It is easy to want to pinch in the throat to begin a vowel because we do when we speak a vowel sound. However, the vowel is not usually spoken with the intensity we put into singing.

This pinching is called a "glottal attack" and can actually "burst" many tiny capillaries in the vocal cords. I am sure you can imagine this is not healthy.

To begin singing a phrase with a vowel does not actually need any focused attack. The mouth can open and the air goes through the vocal cords. No extra effort needs to be given.

If you have a hard time breaking this habit, try to put a tiny puff of air right before the vowel sound that begins a phrase. With practice (and relaxing), in time you won't even need to do this and your sounds will come out effortlessly.

Eeeeeeeasy Does It

Do you notice the childish, anemic sound that comes out when you sing the word "sneak"? This particular vowel problem is unique to Americans and some Asian language sounds. In "American-eeze," we say "E" in a wide, horizontal manner, pulling back the corners of our mouth and almost smile.

In contrast, most European and African languages pronounce the "E" in a vertical, elongated manner. It has more of the character of "if" than "E" to our ears. The "American-eeze" "E" creates the sound in the front of the mouth, using only the area around the upper teeth. Focusing the tone in this small frontal area creates a very shallow, thin sound.

On the other hand, the European "E" uses the entire mouth to resonate the tone, creating a much richer sound that fits much better with the other open vowel sounds we are learning.

Here's the trick: to add depth to a shallow "E," don't even sing "E" but instead sing "ih" (as in "if" or "it"). At the same time you sing a sound that doesn't seem like it would be understandable at all, you *think* an "American-eeze" "E." Simplified, say "ih," think "ee." It's a little tricky at first, but with practice, it will continue to feel more comfortable.

For example, when most Americans speak the word "sneak," the corners of the mouth pull toward the ears, as in an insincere smile. Instead, relax the corners of the mouth and say "snihk" but think "sneek" at the same time. It seems very awkward at first, but with practice, you will notice a difference. By adding depth to the vowel, you are producing a richer sound.

Singing is controlled abandon.
- *unknown*

Chapter 10

Tying it All Together

Go to the Woodshed!

Most people reading this will be too young to remember what a woodshed was, and why sending someone there was so ominous. In "the old days" when most homes were heated with wood, they learned it was not a good idea to keep the wood in the house because it was usually infested with bugs. Therefore, a shed was built a distance from the house where the wood could keep dry, and the bugs would keep out of the house.

The woodshed also became a convenient place to send individuals when whatever sounds they may be making for whatever reason were not welcome in the house. For instance, for many families, the "discipline to the back-side" was done in the woodshed, since the sounds it produced were not conducive to a peaceful home.

Another sound that detracted from the peaceful atmosphere of the home was practicing a musical instrument. Anyone who has successfully played a musical instrument can attest to the monotonous repetition that goes into building musical skills. Their family members can too!

Accomplished musicians have what is called "muscle memory." They have played or sung a piece or difficult passage *correctly* so many times that the nerves can now stimulate the muscles to move with very little conscious thought.

This does not happen without hard work, and concentrated *correct* repetition. That is why I have given you the *Practice Opportunities*. If you only go through them a few times until you feel you understand how to do it correctly, you will only end up being frustrated. To be able to automatically exercise these skills, your muscles must have correct memory. Muscle memory is created by repetition.

Remember, you are just beginning on a new journey. Your muscles and thought patterns have not had much of a chance to develop that very important memory. But, with patience and persistence you will find yourself growing in both ability and confidence.

So, take time each day, if possible, to do the *"Practice Opportunities"* until they are second nature. Don't try to do all of them in one session, but focus on one section at a time. Even after you feel you have internalized a skill, it is always a good idea to regularly go back and refresh yourself in the basics.

A Friend in Deed

It is easy to think we are accomplishing a new skill when, in fact, we may be only masking over old habits. How can you know whether or not you are doing these exercises correctly? The first and most obvious answer would be to find a voice teacher who shares this relaxed view of singing and can assist you in your journey.

If having a teacher or taking a class is not possible, then find a friend who is comfortable in singing and ask them to be your "coach." Be sure to have them read the section you are asking help with, so they are going the same direction you are. If one friend doesn't get it, try another, until you find a combination that "clicks." (This is a good idea when looking for a teacher, too. Not all teachers can teach every individual in the way they need to be taught.)

Joan only had lessons every two weeks, and there were weeks at a time when she couldn't have a lesson at all. Nevertheless, her progress was still very exciting. I would tape Joan's lessons, and she would practice with the tape at home, often not as much as she wanted. Whenever she could practice, she worked hard!

Each week when she returned for another lesson, I could see a clear improvement in the specific areas that Joan practiced. What a joy to see someone come so far in such a short amount of time!

The old saying is "practice makes perfect," and even though we're not trying for perfection, but for joy, the sentiment remains the same. The only way to "unlearn" bad habits and institute new ones is to stick with it, to repeat the new actions over, and over again until they are second nature. So practice any or all of the *Practice Opportunities* whenever you get the opportunity—and just sing *whenever* you get the opportunity!

Natural Resources

The more opportunities you have to sing, the more quickly you will become a singer. By singing, I do not mean necessarily performing for others, but rather singing *with* others. It is sad to say there are so few places to sing for enjoyment in our present culture. Yes, there is the "7th Inning Stretch" and "The Star Spangled Banner" at ball games, but this does not provide the community and acceptance that is enjoyed around the world.

The one exception is a worship service in a church or synagogue. Houses of worship are the only places I am aware of that invite participatory singing. I encourage you to seek out a place where you are comfortable, and can participate.

I find that the children who grow up in homes where singing is not present, but who do attend worship regularly, still gain much more of the ear needed for singing. I am aware of many churches that open up their choir for anyone who wants to sing, with no auditions. That is a *great* way to grow musically!

Of course, singing along with the radio is a favorite pastime, especially when you are driving in your car with the windows up. Just remember that the voices you are hearing on the radio or CD are not real, while *yours* is.

As you sing in this environment, I encourage you to be aware of the tension from driving that can enter across the shoulders and into the upper chest and throat. To release the tension, just do the resting breath exercises, allowing your shoulders, upper chest, throat, and jaw muscles release as you slowly and deeply breath. You can have a much healthier commute in many ways!

However, even better than singing with the radio or a CD, is singing *without* any electronic devices. As you sing by yourself and exercise your musical ear, you'll begin to develop a much more independent singing ability, and your voice will likely be more unique to you. When we sing with recordings, the tendency is to try to imitate the sound of the performer's voice, instead of growing our own.

The best place to sing, I think, is the shower, and it's even socially acceptable! In the shower, you are relaxed, the throat is moist, and the acoustics are fantastic! By acoustics, I mean the close smooth walls, which create a great place for your voice to resonate even more, as the sound bounces off the smooth, enclosed surfaces.

The principle of acoustics is also the reason that when you sing outdoors, even in a large crowd, it feels like you are singing alone. This is because there are no close surfaces for your personal sounds to reverberate against, and the sound of your voice seems so stark and exposed. The happy fact is, that everyone else around you is experiencing the same vocal isolation, so very few would hear your voice anyway! So sing away!

Either sing together with your family and friends at home, or you can go out for karaoke. Sing with children, helping them to find their musical ears, echoing each other back and forth—be sure to affirm them whenever they hit notes right, but make sure they know that whatever they do is great, so that they aren't stunted musically as you might have been.

Around the world, personal singing is the norm, not the exception. Remember, it is play, it is not performance, so, relax, hear the sounds in your head, and *sing!*

Don't be Boxed

As with any growing process, musical development will become frustrating at times and you may well feel like you aren't making any progress, that your voice is beyond hope and you want to give up. **Don't do it!** Take a break; go back to an exercise or song that you feel good about singing. There is always another option, and throwing in the towel only leaves you with a sense of failure on top of failure. Above all, it is not necessary.

With all of my private music students, if I sense their growth is being hampered by their frustrations or expectations, I set up a "bad mouth box." Whenever they say anything negative about their ability, I stop, put a mark in the box, and then refuse to go on until they can tell me a truth that completely and utterly negates what they just said. For instance, if they, in frustration, declare "my voice sounds awful!" I won't go on until

Chapter 10: Tying It All Together

they say something like, "my voice is as unique as my fingerprint, and it is beautiful."

This is generally very hard for people at first, but I've never had to put more than two marks in anyone's "box." However, I have seen that people who do not work hard at changing their thought patterns about their voice, soon get discouraged with their voice, and give up. Without a positive attitude, practice and repetition will prove impossible, and without practice and repetition, your voice will never become the voice that it was meant to be.

There is a common saying among those who work in theater around Broadway in New York City: "It takes seven years to make a singer." By singer, they mean one who can artistically perform in front of a paying audience with high expectations. Of course, these individuals study and rehearse hard over those seven years, and put out a lot of money for training.

If your goal is to sing and enjoy it, I assure you, it can happen. Take the time, be patient, and then PLAY!

So, remember:

      1. Relax and Breathe

      2. Have an "I CAN" Attitude

      3. Think It, then Sing It

      4. Let the Sound Move!

      5. Consonants Connect the Breath to Sound, and Open Up!

      6. Learn the "Tricks of the Trade"

      7. Over, and Over, and Over....

      8. Sing, sing, sing!

      And ----------- DON'T GIVE UP!

---

1. See "Appendix B" (p. 71) for an index to all of the Practice Opportunities in this book.

Epilogue...Joan

After coming to me for lessons off and on over a year and a half, Joan's life became too busy to continue. She had accomplished a tremendous amount with her voice and she could now sing with confidence and joy in church, with her grandchildren, with preschoolers, and whenever else she wanted to.

Joan would never have landed a record contract, appeared on Broadway, or even sung a solo in her church, but that was never her goal. All she wanted to do was sing for joy.

She called me a little over a year later to let me know she was thinking of me. She also told me that she had recently discovered that she had cancer. It had spread to her lungs, she told me, and she was having trouble breathing. Not only that, but she couldn't sing anymore. "But because of what you taught me, Ruth," she confided with great joy, "I still can sing in my head and in my heart—I can hear the music inside."

Joan died a year and a half later and I'm sure she's now one of the most gifted and enthusiastic worship leaders in heaven. I can't wait to be in the choir she is directing!

Appendix A:
Non-Singer to Singer Stories

Appendix A: Non-Singer to Singer Stories

Some readers may still not believe it is possible to grow musically once they have been labeled as "not musical." The following stories are true, most written by the "non-singer-become-singers" themselves. Read on and be encouraged. If you have a story to tell, contact me. I would love to include it in the next printing. (ruth@joyofmusicco.com)

"If I Can, Anyone Can"

In my humble opinion, anyone can learn to sing. Because, if I can do it, anyone can. A brief history: I play guitar, but I wasn't "born musical." In fact, growing up I didn't even listen to music.

I decided that I was going to learn to play guitar…not because I loved music, or always wanted to or anything spectacular like that…I wanted to learn because it was the "one thing my brother couldn't do."

My singing however, was a different story. I had one note and even that was off-key. I was terrible. Everyone told me that I couldn't sing and to give up… everyone except my Mom. She told me to keep trying and often told me what I was doing wrong… and that was a lot.

Day after day, week after week, month after month my poor mother listened patiently as I tortured her with my singing. Bit by bit I became better. Through lots (and I mean lots) of practice and a mother who would never tell me I was doing good unless I really was (she didn't believe in false hopes, she believed in helping someone instead) I eventually became pretty good.

Her constructive criticism helped me learn to sing. I learned that I loved music and that I loved to write songs. I started playing drums, bass, keyboards…anything that I could get my hands on I tried.

Not wanting to brag, but one of my songs was picked as the song of the month for a magazine and I was asked to sing it solo in a concert. I was asked to sing a solo in my church, performing another song that I wrote. I have played with a couple of bands as the lead singer and have worked for several years as a one-man act.

So when I say, "If I can do it, anyone can," I really mean it. Singing and anything else that doesn't come "naturally" to a person can be learned, if you *really* want to learn. You may wish upon a star, but if you don't practice, you'll be forever wishing.

Kenn Crawford, Children's music performer. Used with permission

---

"She Told Me I Must Be Tone Deaf"

When I was in fourth grade our music teacher made me come up to the front of the room (during class) and put my ear to the back of the piano while she pounded the note she wanted me to sing. Needless to say I did not match the pitch. She told me (still in front of the class) that I must be tone deaf.

Later that same year she told me that since I could not master the recorder (her words) I would not be able to play a band instrument. Luckily, that was not her decision.

At the time, I didn't really know what she meant. I was more crushed by her telling me that I wouldn't be able to play the trumpet. (I was a trumpet major in college). I think I just really wanted to play and worked hard at it. I didn't have any trouble.

Now today I am a music teacher (vocal and instrumental). I cringe when anyone calls a child tone deaf. Some children learn to match pitch later than others and the more pressure a child is under the less likely he is to learn. Music should never be a cause of stress for young children.

Sandra L. Greene, Music Director, Cooper County Schools, Used with permission

---

I was Forced to Stand Up in Front... and Sing

In second grade I was forced to stand up in front of the class and try to sing a solo. I would not sing in front of anyone for years after. I ached to join the select chorus in 4th grade and tried out in 4th, 5th, and 6th grades only to be cut each and every year. Finally in 6th grade the elementary music teacher put her arm around me and told me to join the band if I wanted to make music!!

Today I am in my 22nd year of teaching music (nine years instrumental music and 13 years elementary general music). My kids chuckle when I tell them my story.

Jan, Elementary, Music Teacher, Used with permission

"I Found I Could Sing After All!"

For the first 49 years of my life, I was very uncomfortable and self-conscious in any situation where I had to sing with others. I knew I wasn't matching everyone else and couldn't figure out how to get there.

My wife finally convinced me I could learn, so I went to Joy of Music Co. I was surprised to discover my voice capable of quite a range of notes. When I was taught to listen and match notes, I found I could sing after all! A new world was opened up for me after all those years.

It has been so exciting for my wife and me now as we sit next to each other in church. We can sing together! When we go to social events where we participate in a-cappella singing, my voice blends with everyone else's. I can truly enjoy what others have experienced – the joy of singing!"

Dennis Coerber, one of Ruth's students, Used with permission

Eminent Music Professor, Researcher, and Performer was a "Blackbird!"

Dr. Edwin Gordon is an internationally recognized leader in the area of how children learn music. As a fourth-grade child, he was in the general music class at Rogers School in Stamford, Connecticut. Music instruction in the elementary grades at Rogers School were organized around listening to recordings of classical music and occasional performances of class singing accompanied by the assembly-hall piano.

At one point during Edwin's fourth-grade school year, the music specialist, Miss Zillah Lord, required each fourth grader to sing a solo of 'The Battle Hymn of the Republic' as she accompanied on the piano. Evidently, Miss Lord used the quality of the student's performance to decide who the real singers were and who were not.

Edwin attempted to sing this very difficult song in front of the class and his teacher, but it was a struggle. When it was time for group singing, he was then told to join a group of students at the back of the classroom. Miss Lord informed these children that they were part of the "blackbird" group, while the other children were labeled bluebirds.

During group singing, Miss Lord instructed the blackbirds to move only their lips and to leave the singing to the bluebirds. This designation to lip-sync was a traumatic event for Edwin. He felt intimidation, embarrassment, and humiliation. Dr. Gordon now firmly believes that this painful event significantly hindered his musical development.

Musical growth was neither stressed nor encouraged by either of Edwin's parents during his upbringing. However, he does give his mother credit for his young desires to pursue music. He remembers attending the Metropolitan Opera with her a few times during his early years in school. Watching the orchestra perform with the opera sparked his interest in the string bass, which later began his path into music as a vocation.

His mother died suddenly when he was 14. Without her stabilizing presence, he soon got into some mild trouble with a few of his friends from town. His father realized that Edwin had an inclination toward mischief, so he encouraged his son to become involved in something worthwhile.

The suggestion came up that he study music, so Edwin vowed to stay out of trouble if his father bought him a string bass, the instrument that had intrigued him as a young boy. His father agreed, bought his son a bass, and found a local teacher to give him private lessons.

As Edwin received instruction and applied himself, his musicianship quickly improved, and he was soon able to perform in small pick-up groups around Stamford plus the high school band and orchestra. It was during his high school years (1941–1945) that he began to come into his own as a young musician. At the same time, he began to show an interest in a career as a professional musician.

Playing the string bass demands a well-developed musical ear. There are no buttons or keys to push. The musician must learn to play using the ear to tell if the correct note is being played. In addition, playing jazz demands the ability to hear the structure of the music, and play with the structure, many times without any written music to guide.

Edwin took his music studies seriously and in 1942, at the age of 15 he began leaving school early to travel by train some 35 miles to Manhattan. When that lesson was done, he traveled to Long Island for another lesson. These two lessons each week gave him the incredible opportunity to study both classical bass with a bassist with the NBC Orchestra, and jazz with the bassist from Benny Goodman's' band.

After high school, he joined the army and played with the 302nd US Army Band, then went on to attend the prestigious Eastman School of Music. He earned two Master's degrees and a PhD in music. He has played bass in the bands of many jazz greats, and been a popular music education professor at several major universities. Most importantly, through 30 years of research, he developed the groundbreaking Music Learning Theory that is revolutionizing the way music will be taught for future generations.

Through the succeeding years, Dr. Gordon's hard work created a path into musical notoriety and success. Looking back, his frustration about his own musical development was an important piece that shaped his thoughts about music teaching, music learning, and the need to teach to individual differences among all music students.

Those who have had the privilege of learning from Dr. Gordon will agree that his singing voice is not perfect performance quality. But that is not important. His musical ear has grown so much through his work that he sings difficult patterns from, not only our common major and minor scales, but also from the more challenging but beautiful modes. He has also written many lovely melodies that are being used to help children better develop their musical ears.

Edwin E. Gordon, PhD, is a noted teacher, lecturer, author, and researcher in music education and the psychology of music. He has presented at national and international scholarly gatherings numerous papers and lectures on the Music Learning Theory with critical acclaim. He has authored more than twelve books based on groundbreaking research in how children learn music, and has been featured in USA Today and on NBC's Today Show for his innovations in music education.

Dr. Gordon has also been the recipient of many significant awards as a music educator, and has been inducted into the Music Educator's National Conference Hall of Fame. He and several close colleagues founded the Gordon Institute for Music Learning in 1986. The GIML has become an important resource for those desiring to better equip themselves as music educators.

Miss Lord, I am sure, had no idea what an incredible man she identified as a non-singer. I am sure she also had no idea what her ill informed and painful instruction fostered. Dr. Gordon stated recently that the humiliating event in Miss Lord's classroom gave him the desire to make sure other children would not experience the same trauma in their music learning experiences.

Thank you, Dr. Gordon, for not allowing yourself to be limited by an inappropriate label. Instead, you have had the courage follow your desires and the willingness to work hard to learn significant musical and academic skills. Your hard work is now paving the way for many more in future generations to become confident, informed, joyful music makers.

Sources:
The author's conversations and classes with Dr. Gordon, August 4-5, 2001 and July 7-12, 2002; email May 10, 2003.

Gerhardstein, Ronald C. "Edwin E. Gordon: A Biographical and Historical Account of an American Music Educator and Researcher." Ph.D. dissertation. Temple University, 2001. pp. 20-21, 23-27, 29, 31,33, 36, 39, 87, 90-91, 94

Appendix B:
Practice Opportunities Index

Appendix B: Practice Opportunities Index

#1. "Processing the Pain"...... 16

#2. "A Place of Rest"........... 25

#3. "Progressive Relaxation"............. 26

#4. "Affirmations"............. 38

#5. "Spoken Intonation"..................... 42

#6. "Beginning Audiation....................43

#7. "Audiating Intonation"................. 44

#8. "Nya-Nya Play-Song".................. 46

#9. "Moving Upstairs"....................... 51

#10. "The Contented Sigh"................. 52

#11. "The Crow"................................. 52

#12. "The Sssssnake"......................... 55

#13. "The Jumping Sssssnake".......... 56

#14. "Percussive Power".................... 57

#15. "Open Up"................................. 57

#16. "Pure Vowels"........................... 59

Appendix C:

Common Songs to Build a Unified Voice

Appendix C: Common Songs to Build a Unified Voice

Traditional
A Bicycle Built for Two (Daisy, Daisy) – Dacre
Away in a Manger – Murray
Beautiful Dreamer – Foster
Camptown Races – Foster
Come Follow – Traditional English Round
Crawdad Song – African American Folk Song
Deck the Halls – Traditional Welsh Carol
Down by the Riverside – African American Spiritual
Every Time I Feel the Spirit – African American Spiritual
For He's A Jolly Good Fellow - Traditional
The Fox – British Ballad
Go Tell It on the Mountain – African American Spiritual
Green Grow the Rushes – English Folk Song
Hail! Hail! The Gang's All Here – Morse/Sullivan
Heaven Is So High – African American Spiritual
He's Got the Whole World in His Hands – African American Spiritual
Hey Lollee – West Indian Folk Song
I Dream of Jeanie With the Light Brown Hair – Foster
I Love the Mountains – American Folk Song
Jingle Bells – Pierpont
Joy to the World – Handel/Mason/Watts
Oh, Dear, What Can the Matter Be? – English Folk Song
The Sidewalks of New York (Eastside, Westside) – Lawlor/Blake
O, Sinner Man – American Folk Hymn
Sometimes I Feel Like a Motherless Child – African American Spiritual
Standing in the Need of Prayer – African American Spiritual
The Streets of Laredo – Anglo-American Ballad
This Old Man – Traditional English Children's Song
We Three Kings – Hopkins
White Coral Bells – Traditional English
Yankee Doodle – Traditional American

1920's, 1930's, and 1940's
Ballin' the Jack – Burris/Smith
Blue Moon – Rodgers/Hart
Honeysuckle Rose – Waller/Razaf
I'm A Yankee Doodle Dandy – Cohen
I'm Looking Over a Four Leaf Clover – Dixon/Woods
In My Merry Oldsmobile – Edwards/Bryan
The Lady Is a Tramp – Rodgers/Hart
Mairzy Doats – Drake/Hoffman/Livingston
Music, Music, Music (Put Another Nickel In) – Weiss/Baum
Pennies From Heaven – Johnston/Burke
Red Sails In The Sunset – Williams/Kennedy
Singing in the Rain – Brown/Freed

Three Little Fishies (Boop-Boop Dit-tem Dat-tem What-tem Chu!) – Dowell
Toyland – Herbert/MacDonough
Thanks For the Memory – Robin/Rainger
Wooly Bully – Samudio
Yakety Yak (Don't Talk Back) – Leiber/Stoller
Yes, We Have No Bananas – Silver/Cohn
You're A Grand Old Flag – Cohen
The Wiffenpoof Song (Baa! Baa! Baa!) – Minnigerode/Vallee
Whispering – Schonberger/Coburn/Rose

1950's and 1960's
A White Sport Coat (And a Pink Carnation) – Robbins
Alley Cat Song – Harlen/Bjorn
As Long As He Needs Me – Bart
Blowin' in the Wind – Dylan
California Dreamin' – Phillips
Fly Me to the Moon – Howard
Get Together – Powers
Hang On Sloopy – Russell/Knight
Hey, Good Lookin' – Williams
It's Raining – Stookey/Yarrow
King of the Road - Miller
Love Is a Many Splendored Thing – Fain/Webster
Love is Blue – Blackburn/Cour/Popp
Monday, Monday – Phillips
My Special Angel – Duncan
Puff the Magic Dragon – Yarrow/Lipton
Release Me – Miller/Stevenson
Singin' the Blues - Endsley
The Sound of Music – Rodgers/Hammerstein
Sugartime (Sugar in the mornin', sugar in the evenin') – Phillips/Echols
That's Life – Kay/Gordon
Those Were the Days – Raskin
Three Coins in a Fountain – Styne/Cahn
Try to Remember – Jones/Schmidt
Walk Right In – Cannon/Woods
The Wild Side of Life – Warren/Carter

1970's, 1980's, and 1990's
A Horse With No Name – Bunnell
Bad Boy Leroy Brown – Croce
Born at the Right Time - Simon
Born Free – Black/Barry
Bridge Over Troubled Water – Simon
City of New Orleans – Goodman
Everything is Beautiful – Stevens
Friends – Smith/Smith
Further to Fly – Simon
Head Over Heels – Overstreet/Davis
Heartache Tonight – Henley/ Frey/Seger/Souther
Here I Am (Just When I Thought I Was Over You) – Sallitt
Hold Me – McVie/Patton
If – Gates
If You Could Read My Mind – Lightfoot
Inseparable – Jackson/Yancy
Longer – Fogelberg

Lullaby (Goodnight, My Angel) - Joel
Memory – Lloyd Webber/Nunn/Eliot
Mofo – Bono/The Edge
The Obvious Child - Simon
Running On – Winwood/Jennings
Saved By Zero – Curnin/Greenall/woods/West-Oram/Agius
Southern Nights – Toussaint
Still Waters Run Deep – Gibb/Gibb/Gibb
Straight and Narrow – Overstreet/Schlitz
Tears in Heaven – Clapton/Jennings
Thank You – McCary/Morris/Stockman/Austin
Till the Answer Comes – Overstreet/Carpenter/Prince
Vibin' – Morris/Morris/Stockman/Robinson
The Way It Is – Hornsby
You Got It – Orbison/Lynne/Petty
You Make Me Feel Like Dancing – Sayer/Ponica
You'll Keep On Searching – Winwood/Jennings
You're So Vain – Simon

Children's
A-Tisket A-Tasket – Traditional American
Be Kind to Your Web-Footed Friends – Miller/Sousa
The Bunny Hop – Anthony/Auletti
Hot Cross Buns – Traditional English
How Much is that Doggie in the Window? – Merrill
I'm Popeye the Sailor Man – Lerner
John Jacob Jingleheimer Schmidt – Traditional American
London Bridge – Traditional English
My Dog's Bigger Than Your Dog – Paxton
Oats, Peas, Beans and Barley Grow – Traditional American
Oh Where, Oh Where Has My Little Dog Gone? – Traditional American
Pussy-cat, Pussy-cat – Traditional English
Who's Afraid of the Big Bad Wolf – Churchill

Sacred Choruses
All Hail King Jesus! – Moody
Bind Us Together
Bless His Holy Name – Crouch
Blessed Be the Name of the Lord – Moen
The Celebration Song – Chambers
Everything's Gonna Be Alright – Poken
The Family of God – Gaither
Fear Not – Pringle
Give Thanks – Smith
God of Wonders – Myrd/Hindalong
Hallelujah (Shout to the Earth) – Reardon
He Keeps Me Singing (There's Within My Heart) – Bridgers
Here I Am to Worship – Hughes
His Name Is Wonderful – Meir
I Could Sing of Your Love Forever – Smith
I'm Trading My Sorrows – Evans
In Him We Live – Speir
In the Lord Alone – Harrah
I Will Bless the Lord – Hernandez
Jesus is All the World to Me – Thompson
Jesus, Name Above All Names – Hearn

Jesus, Lover of My Soul – Oakley
Jesus Loves the Little Children – Root
Let the Walls Fall Down – Blatstone/Barbour/Barbour
Majesty – Hayford
Open the Eyes Of My Heart – Baloche
Pour Out Your Spirit – Lane
Some Golden Daybreak – Blackmore
Spirit of the Living God – Iverson
Strength of My Life – Phillips
Surely the Presence of the Lord Is in This Place – Wolfe
The Joy of the Lord is My Strength – Vale
There's Something About That Name – Gaither
Through It All – Crouch
Thy Loving Kindness – Mitchell
Unto Thee, O Lord – Monroe
Victory Chant – Vogels
We Bring the Sacrifice of Praise – Dearman
We Want to See Jesus Lifted High – Horley
What A Mighty God We Serve – Traditional
Worthy, You Are Worthy – Moen
You Are the Rock of My Salvation – Muller
You're Worthy of My Praise – Ruis

Hymns
A Mighty Fortress is Our God – Luther
Come Thou Almighty King – de Giardini
Down at the Cross – Stockton/Hoffman
Faith is the Victory – Sankey
He the Pearly Gates Will Open – Ahlwen
Hiding In Thee – Sankey
I Am Thine, O Lord – Doane/Crosby
Joyful, Joyful, We Adore Thee – Beethoven/van Dyke
Leaning on the Everlasting Arms – Showalter/Hoffman
Now Thank We All Our God – Cruger/Rinkart
O Come, All Ye Faithful – Wade
O Jesus, I Have Promised – Mann/Bode
O Little Town of Bethlehem – Redner
Pass Me Not, O Gentle Savior – Doane/Crosby
Standing On the Promises – Johnson/Carter
'Tis So Sweet to Trust in Jesus – Kirkpatrick/Stead
What a Friend We Have in Jesus – Converse/Scriven
Wonderful Words of Life – Bliss